500 *Sewing* Tips, Tricks, Techniques, and Hacks

---- Ashley Hough ----

Must-Have Manual for Easy and Accurate Sewing

500 Sewing Tips, Tricks, Techniques, and Hacks

Landauer Publishing, *www.landauerpub.com,* is an imprint of Fox Chapel Publishing Company, Inc.

Copyright © 2025 by Ashley Hough and Fox Chapel Publishing Company, Inc.

All rights reserved. No part of this book may be reproduced, stored in a retrieval system, or transmitted in any form or by any means, electronic, mechanical, photocopying, recording, or otherwise, without the prior written permission of Fox Chapel Publishing, except for the inclusion of brief quotations in an acknowledged review and the enlargement of the template patterns in this book for personal use only. The patterns themselves, however, are not to be duplicated for resale or distribution under any circumstances. Any such copying is a violation of copyright law.

Project Team
Acquisitions Editor: Amelia Johanson
Editor: Madeline DeLuca
Designer: Mike Deppen
Proofread & Index: Jean Bissell
Photographer: Ashley Hough

Shutterstock.com photographs and images: PawLoveArt (illustrations: back cover, 8, top right thimble, 45, 49, 139, 145 buttons,165, 226); Moonnoon (illustrations: back cover, 10 bottom right thimble,128, 204, 235 green thread, 254, 280); Glinskaja Olga (illustrations: 3, 13); Simol1407 (6–7); Pedal to the Stock (11, bottom photo); Syana Artfanat (11, illustration); vik.stock (illustrations: 10 top thimble,15, 113); Olena Illustrations (illustrations: 12, 19, 97 iron); AnnaKoles (illustrations: 21, 278); Alina. Alina (33 illustration); Freeograph (34–35); Edge Creative (illustrations: 36, 245); Nadiyka U (illustrations: 50, 68); ClassicVector (70, illustration); Keronn art (illustrations: 80, 264); Planet OfVectors (88, illustration); mentalmind (illustrations: 92, 100, 106, 121); NataLyaroArt (illustrations: 86, 96); Natalia Hoffmann (97 bottom right illustration); Sata Production (116–117, 123); Rawpixel. com (19 illustration); GoodStudio (illustrations: 118, 156, 192, 277); Sensvector (illustrations: 124, 279); Sofija29 (154–155); Kit8. net (illustrations: 158, 185, 235 bottom right); GN Studio (176, illustration); cosmaa (186, illustration); Alena TS (202–203); lemono (206, illustration); Nattika (212–213); S_I_0_0_P (215 bottom right); designium (224–225); PetiteARTist (230, illustration); Kostikova Natalia (236–237); SanaStock (238); Organic Shots Studio (239 cashmere photo); Apugach (photos: 240 eyelet, 246 rayon); Prozo (243 leather photo); Tom Gowanlock (245 photo); Ryan Garrett (246 seersucker photo) Katerina Maksymenko (terrycloth photo); inspiring.team (247, illustration); everydayplus (249 wool photo); Rumka vodki (249, illustration); Samuel perales (250–251); robertsre (252, photo); Amanita Silvicora (252, illustration).

ISBN 978-1-63981-123-6

Library of Congress Control Number: 2025942282

To learn more about the other great books from Fox Chapel Publishing, or to find a retailer near you, call toll-free 800-457-9112 or visit us at *www.FoxChapelPublishing.com.*

We are always looking for talented authors.
To submit an idea, please send a brief inquiry to acquisitions@foxchapelpublishing.com.
Or write to:
Fox Chapel Publishing
903 Square Street
Mount Joy, PA 17552

Printed in China
First printing

This book has been published with the intent to provide accurate and authoritative information in regard to the subject matter within. While every precaution has been taken in the preparation of this book, the author and publisher expressly disclaim any responsibility for any errors, omissions, or adverse effects arising from the use or application of the information contained herein.

Welcome!

To me, sewing is one of those skills that you can always expand. Whether it's learning a new or different construction technique, altering pattern pieces to make garments that better fit your body, trying out different seam finishes, or simply learning about a fabric, tool, or notion that you didn't know existed, there can always be something new.

I learned to sew at a young age from my mom. I remember her fixing work shirts for my dad, sewing prom dresses for my sister, and making other projects for around the house. Sitting on the counter in our laundry room, I watched and eventually got to help pin patterns to fabric, cut pieces out, then help with simple straight sewing—sitting on her lap with a box under the pedal so I could reach it.

It's been quite a few years since then, and I've gathered a fair bit of knowledge over that time. In this book, I'm excited to share that knowledge with you! We'll explore the seemingly endless amounts of different fabrics, needles, and thread, and better understand when to use what. I'll also share a long list of tools, notions, and sewing machine feet—all of which can make certain sewing processes quicker and easier! And, for those of you who like sewing without a machine, I'll cover hand-sewing stitches and smocking. Plus, there are tons of time-saving tips, great tricks, and fun hacks that you can start using in your sewing room right away!

Whether you've been sewing for years or you're just starting out, I truly hope this book has something for everyone!

–Ashley Hough

Table of Contents

Tools 6
Techniques 34
Patterns 116
Closures 126
Finishing Techniques 154
Hand Sewing 202
Needle Knowledge 212
Thread Theory 224
Fabric Facts 236
Fabric Form & Function 250
Index 276
About the Author 280

Tools

The sewing world is filled with dozens and dozens, if not hundreds, of sewing tools; everything from must-have tools like scissors and pins, to those that can make certain aspects of sewing easier, like a thread conditioner for hand sewing. There are even some tools that you may not have known existed, like a buttonhole spacer or a hump jumper, or those that you have probably seen but maybe not known what they are for, like the "strawberry" on a pincushion. Here is a collection of some of the most used and useful of these sewing tools.

Pins	8
Thimbles	10
Measuring Tools	12
Marking Tools	13
Cutting Tools	15
Pressing Tools	19
Additional Tools	21
Sewing Machine Feet	27

Pins

Not all pins are created equal. Just like there are different needles for different fabric types and applications, there are different pins too. Picking the right pin will help ensure that no matter what you are sewing, whether it's different types of fabric, upholstery repair, or sequins, it will be securely held in place.

Straight Pin

A standard straight pin can be used on most woven fabrics. They come in different lengths and thicknesses to accommodate lighter- and heavier-weight fabric.

Ballpoint Pin

Ballpoint pins should be used on knit or other stretch fabrics. They have a slightly rounded point that can go in between the fabric fibers, rather than piercing through them, which

will reduce the risk of a pin snagging or creating a run in the fabric.

Silk Pin

Silk or satin pins should be used when sewing with silk, satin, or other delicate fabrics.

They are very sharp and fine and won't leave holes or marks in the fabric like a standard straight pin could.

Appliqué Pin

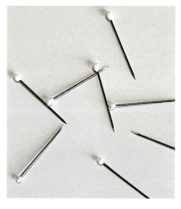

Appliqué pins are very short pins with a small or tapered head. The shorter length allows you to place more pins around the edge of a small appliqué shape without the pin ends overlapping. The small or tapered head won't catch on the thread as easily if you are hand sewing the pieces in place.

Fork Pin

Fork pins are like placing two pins at one time, so they are extra secure. They also have a curved end, which makes them easier to insert into fabric that is lying flat on a surface.

T-Pin

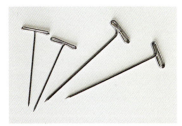

T-pins are aptly named because their head resembles the letter T. T-pins are great to use when pinning through buttonholes or when blocking lace or another open or loosely woven embellishment. They can also be used when doing upholstery, as there is no chance of the pin accidentally getting pushed through into a piece of furniture as could happen with a small-head pin.

Basting Pin

Basting pins are essentially curved safety pins. These are great to use when holding  multiple layers of fabric together, like when basting a quilt, and the curved bottom makes them easier to insert into the fabric while it is lying flat on a surface.

Glass-Head Pin

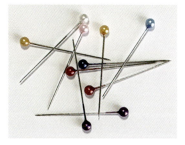

Glass-head pins should be used any time you may be ironing or steaming fabric near the pins, as plastic head pins could melt.

Flat-Head Pin

Flat head pins are great to use any time you are hand sewing,

Trick!

A glass-head pin on a pressing surface can help you quickly and easily make single-fold tape! Insert the pin under a small section of the pressing mat, leave a space the width that you want the final tape to be, then insert the pin tip into the pressing mat again.

Cut a strip of fabric that is twice the pin space in width. At one end of the fabric strip, fold the raw edges toward the center and press, then insert the pressed end under the pin. Pull the fabric under the pin and press it as you pull it out. The fabric edges will be folded toward the center as it passes under the pin.

as the thread is less likely to catch on the head.

Flexible-Head Pin

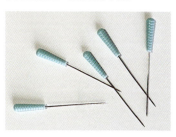

Flexible-head pins have long, flexible heads usually made of rubber or another easy-to-grip material that can bend slightly.

Thimbles

When it comes to hand sewing, thimbles are finger savers! Whether you are sewing through heavier-weight fabrics and need the extra help pushing the needle through the fabric layers, or you are hand quilting a large project and want to spare your fingers from repeatedly pushing and pulling the needle through the multiple layers of a quilt, thimbles are the answer.

Metal Thimble

A standard metal thimble is one of the most recognizable types of thimble. It fits on the end of your finger and offers the most amount of protection possible. Many metal thimbles also have a ring or "lip" around the upper edge, as well as many small indentations on the upper edge and sides. These allow the end of a needle to fit into one of those indentations or rest along the lip and not slip around.

Silicone Thimble

A silicone thimble is a flexible thimble that fits more snuggly around the end of

your fingertip. It protects the fingertip when pushing a needle through fabric and offers extra grip when pulling a needle through fabric.

Leather Thimble

A leather thimble is a flexible thimble made of leather that fits snuggly on your fingertip. Generally, they have a small circle of metal with

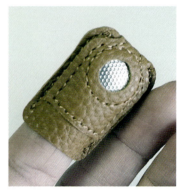

indentations that help keep the needle end from slipping as you push it through fabric.

Sticky Thimble

A sticky thimble is a small adhesive patch that can be stuck to the tip of your finger to protect your finger when pushing a needle though fabric. Sticky thimbles can be found as either single use or reusable.

Open Thimble

An open thimble has either an open top or open back, both

of which allow room for a longer fingernail.

Ring Thimble

A ring thimble is an adjustable metal ring with small

indentations. It can be worn on any finger and used to push a needle through fabric.

Thimbles are helpful when pushing the needle through fabric and for sparing your fingers from needle pricks!

Measuring Tools

Whether you are making pillows and other home décor items, or shirts, jackets, and other garments, you're going to need a variety of measuring tools. Using the right type of measuring tool for your application will ensure you get accurate numbers and your project turns out as intended.

Fiberglass Measuring Tape

A flexible fiberglass measuring tape is used to take body measurements when sewing garments. The tape is flexible enough to bend around any part of the body, but also won't stretch.

Curved Rulers

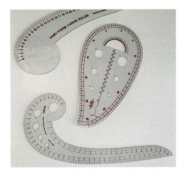

Curved rulers are used when drafting patterns and can help when truing up and drawing in lines like the armscye, neckline, or hip curve areas.

Retractable Measuring Tape

If you are measuring your own body, having a tape that can connect back to itself and then cinch tight can be a big help!

Quilting Rulers

Quilting rulers come in a variety of squares, rectangles, and triangles and are used to

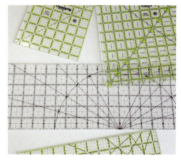

not only measure fabric, but to cut against to get straight lines.

Ruler Grip Tape

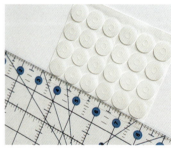

Ruler grip tape can be used to help hold a ruler in place. When using a long ruler for cutting strips, it can be common to find that the ruler slips along the fabric. Grip tape applied to the underside of the ruler can help hold it in place while you cut.

12 500 Sewing Tips, Tricks, Techniques, and Hacks

Marking Tools

Whether you are tracing a complete pattern piece onto fabric to cut it out, or you're marking pocket placements or dart lines, having the right type of marking tool can make the difference. While pretty much anything can make a mark on fabric, the important part can come down to whether that mark is permanent and how it can be removed from fabric.

Air-Soluble Fabric Marker

Marks and lines made using an air-soluble fabric marker will fade away over time. It is always important to test the marker on a scrap piece of fabric first to ensure that any marks fade completely before using it on your project.

Water-Soluble Fabric Marker

Marks and lines made using a water-soluble fabric marker fade when the fabric gets wet. It is always important to test the marker on a scrap piece of fabric first to ensure that any marks completely wash away before using it on your project.

Heat-Erasable Fabric Marker

Marks and lines made using a heat-erasable marker disappear when the fabric is ironed. Always test the marker on a scrap piece of fabric first to ensure that any marks completely disappear when ironed, and of course, only use this marker on fabrics that can be ironed with a warm iron.

Tailor's Chalk

Tailor's chalk is a thin piece of chalk, usually in a triangular shape, used to make marks on fabric, generally when sewing or altering clothing. The chalk can either be brushed away when the mark is no longer needed, or it will disappear when the fabric is washed.

Chalk Sharpener

If you use your tailor's chalk often, eventually it will need to be sharpened. A chalk sharpener allows you to run

the dull edge of the chalk along it to bring it back to a sharper point. Having a sharper point will keep your chalk marks more accurate.

Tracing Wheel and Tracing Paper

A tracing wheel, used in conjunction with tracing paper, can be used to transfer marks from a pattern to fabric. The wheel has "spokes" with blunt tips that poke through the pattern paper and transfer little dots of chalk (or carbon, depending on the tracing paper) onto the fabric underneath. You can also find tracing wheels that

have sharp spokes that are meant to be used without the tracing paper. Rather than transferring dots, they create a line of tiny holes in the fabric. Tracing paper is thin paper that has either chalk or carbon, and when used in conjunction with a tracing wheel, will transfer marks onto fabric. This paper can be found in a variety of colors, allowing you to choose the one that shows up best on your fabric.

Hera Marker

A hera marker is a small, curved tool that makes marks on fabric by making an indentation, rather than leaving behind any kind of ink or chalk.

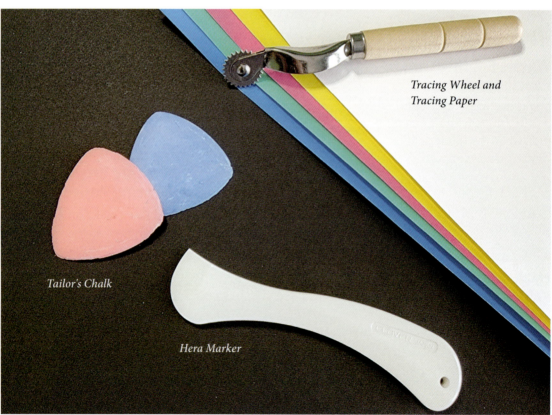

Tracing Wheel and Tracing Paper

Tailor's Chalk

Hera Marker

Cutting Tools

No matter what your sewing project is, a cutting tool is a must-have! From scissors to snips, rotary cutters to pinking shears, there's a tool for every application.

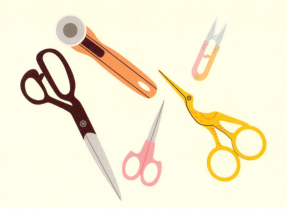

Rotary Cutters

Rotary cutters are round blades used to cut through layers of fabric. Rotary cutters must be used in conjunction with a cutting mat, as there needs to be a surface under the fabric as you cut. Rotary blades come in a variety of different sizes. Smaller rotary blades are great for cutting single layers of thin fabric or cutting around curves, while the larger blades can be used for cutting through multiple layers of bulkier fabric, like fleece or flannel.

Tip!
Using a dull rotary blade can be more dangerous than using a sharp one. When the blade is dull, you are more likely to be pushing harder than necessary on the blade, which could lead to injury. As soon as you notice the blade not cutting a fabric fiber here and there, even if it's just one, you should change the blade.

Tip!
Always close the blade guard on a rotary cutter when you set it down. This will reduce the risk of an accidental cut if you bump your hand into the cutter or accidentally knock it on the floor. If you have a hard time remembering to close the blade guard, consider getting a rotary cutter that automatically closes the blade guard when you let go of the handle.

Specialty Rotary Blades

Specialty rotary blades can be used to cut decorative edges along fabric, such as a wavy or a pinked edge.

Tip!

Never just throw a rotary blade in the trash. If you buy the blades individually, use the plastic container that you take the new blade out of to put the old one in before throwing away. If you don't have an old container, fold a piece of cardboard in half around the blade, and then tape the edges before throwing away.

Tip!

Rotary blades come in several sizes: 18mm, 28mm, 45mm, and 60mm. The smaller 18mm and 28mm blades are great to use when cutting out pattern pieces that have tight curves. The 45mm blades can be used with most fabrics and can cut through several layers at a time. The larger 60mm blades are great to use with bulky or lofty fabrics.

Circle Cutter

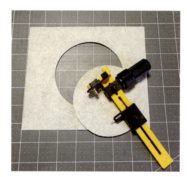

A circle cutter can be used when cutting out circles between 1 ½" (3.8cm) and 8 ¾" (22.2cm) in diameter. Simply place the pivot point into the fabric at the desired circle center, rotate the blade clockwise, and you have a perfect circle cut and ready to use.

Self-Healing Cutting Mat

A self-healing cutting mat protects your table or other

work surface when using a rotary cutter. The self-healing part of the mat allows the mat to come back together after a cut is made so the mat maintains its flat surface.

Rotating Cutting Mat

A rotating cutting mat has a base under the mat that allows it to easily rotate around a center point.

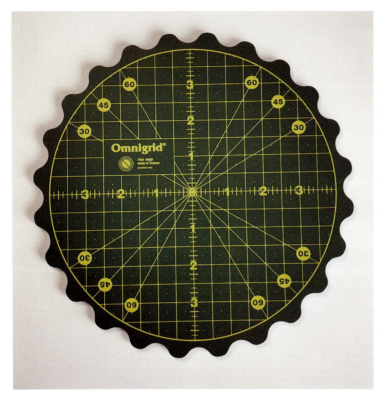

This allows you to make a cut on one or two sides of a piece of fabric, then easily rotate the mat to make more cuts without having to pick up the mat to move it.

Scissors

Scissors come in all shapes and sizes. It's always a good idea to have a sharp pair of scissors with long blades for cutting fabric. When cutting out pattern pieces, it's helpful to have a pair of scissors with a flat blade along the bottom. This allows the scissors to stay closer to the table when going around the pattern pieces. It doesn't lift the fabric as far away from the table, which leads to more accurate cuts. These types of scissors are commonly referred to as fabric shears.

Hack!

Use a small, sticky backed hook on your machine to hold a pair of snips, so you'll always know where they are!

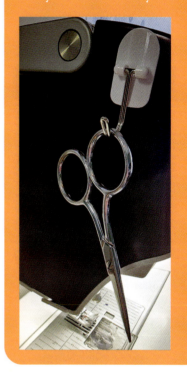

Snips

Snips are small scissors that are meant for snipping threads. These can simply look like a small pair of scissors or be "spring loaded," allowing for easier use.

Pinking Shears

Pinking shears are scissors that have triangular teeth along their blades. Rather than cutting a straight line, they cut small V shapes along the fabric edge. Having a pinked edge can help prevent fabric fraying.

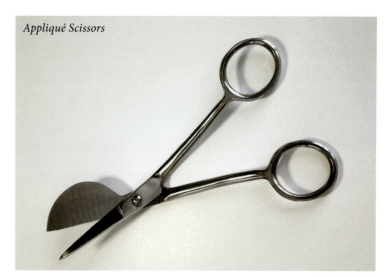

Appliqué Scissors

Appliqué Scissors

Appliqué scissors, sometimes referred to as duck bill scissors, have a wide, flat blade on one side and are slightly angled. They are ideal for trimming a top layer of fabric along an edge of stitching. The wide paddle-like side slides under the top layer of fabric and pushes it up slightly, allowing you to cut close to a line of stitching.

Curved Embroidery Scissors

Curved embroidery scissors are small, sharp scissors meant for trimming threads while doing embroidery, either on the machine or by hand. The bent handle and curved tip design allows you to cut close to the edge of the fabric while keeping the main part of the blades parallel to the fabric. This makes it less likely that you will accidentally snip into the fabric.

Pinking Shears

Pressing Tools

Pressing is an important step in most sewing projects and can help make a project look more professionally done. However, not everything can be pressed the same. From different types of fabrics to the shape of a seam, there's a pressing tool for pretty much any application.

Ironing Board

An ironing board is a long, narrow board that has a taper on one end. It is generally a wooden or metal frame, covered with a slightly padded material and fabric on top. An ironing board is a general-purpose tool that can be used for pressing anything from fabric yardage to garments.

Pressing Mat

A pressing mat is a small, padded pressing surface that can be used to press smaller pieces of fabric. These can be made from the same materials as an ironing board or are commonly made from wool as well. A pressing mat can also be used directly on a tabletop.

Pressing Ham

A pressing ham is a tightly stuffed "pillow" that can be used to press curved seams. These are commonly used when pressing garments in areas like sleeves, or when pressing darts.

Sleeve Pressing Board

A sleeve pressing board looks like a miniature ironing board and is used when pressing sleeves. It can also be used when pressing pant legs. The narrow feature of the board allows for the sleeve or leg opening to easily fit around the board so that it can be pressed without lying flat, which would lead to creases.

Sleeve Pressing Board

Press Cloth

A press cloth is a piece of lightweight material that is placed between the fabric being pressed and the iron. A press cloth is meant to help protect the fabric being pressed from either melting or being marked by the iron in any way.

Teflon Pressing Sheet

A Teflon pressing sheet is a thin piece of Teflon material that is placed between the fabric being pressed and an iron. This non-stick surface protects both the fabric and the iron and can be used when pressing over an area where the iron might "stick" to the surface, like a screen print on a t-shirt. A Teflon pressing sheet can also be used when applying fusible web or interfacing to protect the iron from meeting the adhesive.

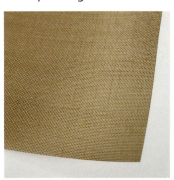

Clapper

A clapper is a wooden block used to create a flat seam. It is generally used in conjunction with a pressing bar or other pressing surface. Steam is applied to the fabric, and then the clapper is placed firmly on top of the seam as it cools, flattening it.

Pressing Bar

A pressing bar is a narrow wooden tool used for pressing narrow seams or seams in hard-to-reach areas like collars.

Pressing Bar

Seam Roller

A seam roller is a small roller that can be used to flatten seams. The roller can be made from either wood or a hardened plastic or rubber. A seam roller is a helpful tool to use on fabrics that cannot take the heat of an iron.

Additional Tools

Beyond the basics, there are lots of small-but-mighty tools that can make sewing faster, easier, and more precise. These tools are helpful, whether you're fine-tuning your techniques, or solving tricky challenges.

Strawberry on a Pincushion

The small strawberry attached to a pincushion is something we've probably all seen at one point or another, but maybe not realized that it has a practical purpose. It is generally stuffed with emery powder, or something similar, and can be used to sharpen the tip of a needle or pin. Emery is an abrasive material (just like the material on a nail file), so when a pin or needle is rubbed against it in the strawberry, it can help remove any burrs from the needle or pin tip and help them more cleanly and easily glide into fabric.

Needle Threaders

A needle threader is a small tool that helps easily slide a length of thread through the eye of a needle. These can come in a variety of different shapes and sizes, but all serve the same purpose. Some even come with built-in lights!

Fray Check

Fray Check is a liquid seam-sealant that can help secure thread ends or keep the edges of fabric from fraying.

Tools / Additional Tools   21

It can be applied along an edge of fabric in a seam, or used to provide extra security to thread ends in areas like buttonholes.

Thread Conditioner

Tread conditioners can help improve the quality of thread when both hand and machine sewing. If you are using a spool of thread on a machine that might be old, applying a liquid thread conditioner to the spool prior to use can improve the strength of the thread and keep it from potentially fraying or breaking. When hand sewing, thread conditioner or wax can be applied to the length of thread to keep it from tangling and knotting unintentionally.

Bobbin Winder

A bobbin winder is a tool that winds thread from a spool onto a bobbin. While most sewing machines have the capability of doing this on the machine, a stand-alone bobbin winder allows you to wind a bobbin without needing to unthread and then rethread your machine. They can be used with a variety of different sizes of both thread spools and bobbins.

Bobbin Buddies

Bobbin buddies are handy tools that help keep a wound bobbin with its matching spool of thread. These are

Hack!

If you're struggling to thread a needle with thicker thread or embroidery floss and don't have any thread conditioner, lip balm can be used in a pinch!

Tip!

1. When winding a bobbin, pull the thread through the small opening at the top of the bobbin before placing it on the machine to wind.

2. Hold the thread as you wind the first bit of thread, then trim the thread tail flush with the top of the bobbin and continue winding. This makes it so there is no small thread tail that could get tangled while you sew, especially as you near the end of the bobbin.

great to use if you regularly use different colors of thread when sewing and are frequently changing out bobbins.

> **Tip!**
> Always turn the handwheel of your machine toward you. Turning it away from you could cause thread tangles in the bobbin area.

Seam Ripper

A seam ripper is a tool used to cut threads and rip out seams. This can be used because a seam was incorrectly sewn, or because you are ripping out a seam to do an alteration to a garment. Seam rippers have two sides: one with a point and one with a ball. The pointed side can be inserted under individual stiches to lift and cut the thread without damaging the fabric. The ball side can be inserted into a seam to allow you to push the seam ripper down the entire

> **Trick!**
> When cutting open buttonholes with a seam ripper, place a straight pin at both ends of the buttonhole to keep yourself from accidentally cutting too far.
>
>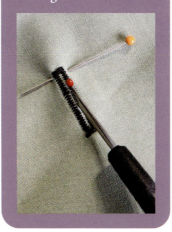

> **Tip!**
> Need to take out a stitching line? If you use a seam ripper on the bobbin side of your stitching line to slice through every fourth or fifth stitch, you can simply pull out the top thread with little effort.

length of a seam, cutting all the threads, while the ball point protects the fabric from being cut.

Stiletto

A stiletto is a sharp, pointed tool that can be used to help hold layers of fabric together when sewing. The stiletto can help keep fabric in place as it goes under the presser foot while keeping your fingers away from the needle.

Seam Gauge

A seam gauge is a tool that allows you to quickly and

Tools / Additional Tools 23

easily measure common seam allowances.

Seam Measurement Guide

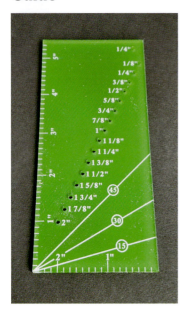

A seam measurement guide allows you to easily mark a desired seam allowance on the throat plate of your machine based on your needle position. To use, simply select the seam allowance measurement you want to use. Using the hand wheel of your machine, lower the needle into the hole next to that measurement. Lower the presser foot to hold the guide in place, then mark the seam allowance on the throat plate of your machine using a magnetic seam allowance guide, tape, or other marking method.

Bodkin

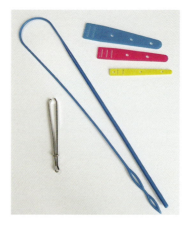

A bodkin is used for pulling elastic, cord, string, or other material through a narrow opening like a waistband or hood edge. Bodkins can come in a variety of different shapes, sizes, and materials. Flat plastic bodkins in various widths can be easily used with different widths of elastic, while metal bodkins with "teeth" are handy to use when gripping the end of a drawstring.

Point-Turning Tool

A point-turning tool helps turn out corners and points on projects. While it is common to want to use a pair of scissors or snips to do this job, a point-turning tool can help you get crisp points without running the risk of accidentally pushing through the fabric.

Hump Jumper

A hump jumper, also called a seam jumper, helps sew over thick areas of fabric. For example, if you are hemming a pair of jeans and need to sew over the layers of fabric from the side seam, the hump jumper can be inserted under the back side of the presser foot to make it level. This helps you avoid skipped or uneven stitches.

Pattern Drafting Paper

Pattern drafting paper is used when drafting or creating new pattern pieces. It comes on rolls, making it great for any size pattern piece from a bodice front to a long pant leg. It is also a semi-transparent paper, which makes it easier to transfer markings from one pattern piece to another or to see lines when transferring alterations.

Hack!
If you struggle to pick up washers or thin pattern weights, make a small fabric bag to go around them so that there's something to grab on to.

Bias Tape Maker

Bias Tape Maker
A bias tape maker is a tool that evenly folds the edges of fabric in toward the center to make bias tape. A strip of fabric is inserted into the larger open end and then pulled out the smaller end and pressed. Bias tape makers come in a variety of different sizes depending on the finished width of tape you are wanting to make.

Fusible Bias Tape Maker
A fusible bias tape maker is very similar to a regular

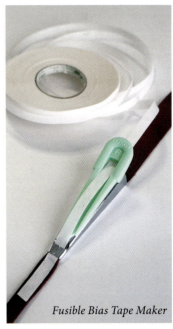

Fusible Bias Tape Maker

Tools / Additional Tools   25

bias tape maker, except that it has an additional opening that allows you to insert a thin strip of fusible web that is adhered to the bias tape as it is folded and pressed. After it is made, the paper side can be removed from the fusible web and the fusible bias tape can be adhered to a project.

Fabric Glue

Fabric glue comes in a variety of different options, from temporary to permanent, and liquid to stick. When selecting the type of glue you use, consider the application and whether you are looking to use the glue to temporarily hold something in place before you sew it, or whether you want to use it in place of sewing something. Also be sure to check whether the glue will dry flexible or stiff, and if it can be sewn through after it dries. Another aspect of glue to consider is whether it dries transparent.

Basting Spray

Basting spray is an adhesive spray used to temporarily hold layers of fabric together before they are stitched.

Buttonhole Spacer

A buttonhole spacer is an expandable tool that

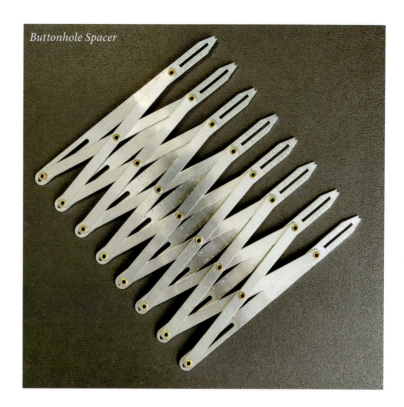

Buttonhole Spacer

allows you to accurately mark evenly spaced lines for buttonholes. It can also be used for evenly marking tucks or pleats.

Buttonhole Cutter

A buttonhole cutter is a thin, straight cutting tool. With a cutting mat or other protective surface under the fabric, the buttonhole cutter can be pressed into the fabric to quickly and easily cut a straight line into the fabric and open the buttonhole after it is stitched.

Sewing Machine Feet

While a lot of sewing can be done with a standard presser foot (the one that comes on the machine when you buy it), other, more specialized feet can not only make certain sewing techniques easier, but make the end result look better.

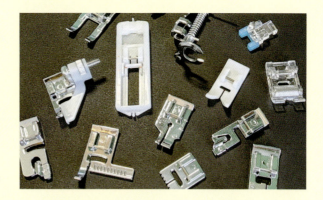

Hack!

Sometimes pieces of dust and lint get further down into the machine than what you can reach with the little cleaning brush that comes with it. Use a pipe cleaner or makeup brush to reach them!

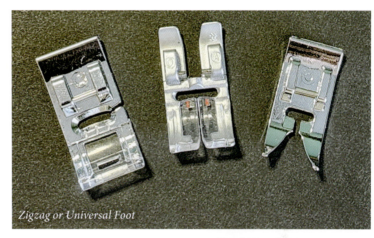
Zigzag or Universal Foot

It has a large oval opening for the needle, allowing you to stitch everything from straight to zigzag, and basic monogram to decorative stitches, all with the same foot. Depending on the brand of foot you have, the look of the opening can differ.

Straight-Stitch Foot

A straight-stitch foot is designed specifically for sewing a straight stitch only. It has a very small hole opening, allowing for use with a straight stitch in the center

Zigzag or Universal Foot

A zigzag foot is one of the most commonly used feet and is often referred to as a standard or universal foot.

needle position. This foot is great to use on lightweight or sheer fabric. The small hole opening helps eliminate puckers in the fabric as you stitch.

Open-Toe Foot

An open-toe foot is a standard presser foot with a large center opening. This

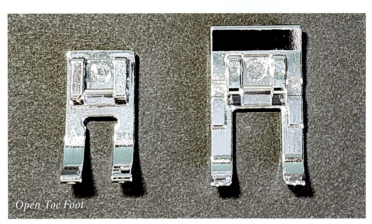
Open-Toe Foot

center opening allows for more visibility of the stitches when doing techniques like appliqué or other decorative stitching. The opening of open-toe feet can come in a variety of widths.

Guide Foot

A guide foot is a standard presser foot with a short

guide, like a built-in ruler on one side. This guide can be used to help keep lines of stitching straight and evenly spaced.

Quarter-Inch Foot

A quarter-inch foot is commonly used in quilting, as that is the standard seam

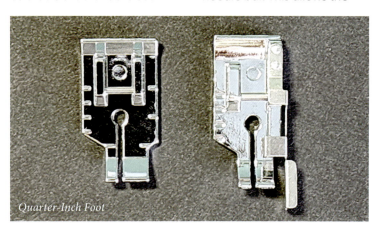
Quarter-Inch Foot

>
> ### Tip!
> Never used compressed air when cleaning your sewing machine. Doing this can force dust, lint, and other little fabric fibers further into the machine.

allowance width. From the center needle position to the edge of the foot measures ¼" (6.4mm). Some quarter-inch feet also have built in guides along the outer edge of the foot that allow you to align the edge of the fabric against it to maintain an accurate ¼" (6.4mm) seam allowance. Many quarter-inch feet also have a horizontal line on the foot indicating where you should stop sewing if you want to be ¼" (6.4mm) away from the edge of the fabric in order to pivot and continue sewing down another side.

Walking Foot

A walking foot is a large presser foot attachment that essentially adds feed dogs to the top of the fabric. In addition to being attached to the machine where traditional feet are attached, it is also attached to the needle bar. This allows the

foot to move up and down in sync with the feed dogs below the fabric. This evenly feeds thick fabric or bulky layers through the sewing machine without puckering. A walking foot is also commonly referred to as an even-feed foot or a dual-feed foot.

Guide Bar

A guide bar, or quilting guide bar, is a thin metal bar that can be attached to a slot or hole in a walking foot. It serves as a visual guide for keeping lines of stitching even and can be adjusted to a variety of different widths between the lines of stitching.

Stitch-in-the-Ditch Foot

A stitch-in-the-ditch foot has a metal guide that runs along the "ditch" or seam between two fabrics, allowing you

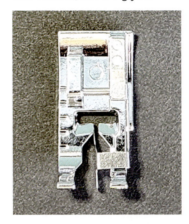

to sew directly in the ditch, keeping the stitches hidden. This is a common quilting technique, but can also be used when edge joining two pieces of fabric and can be referred to as an edge-joining foot.

Free-Motion Foot

A free-motion quilting foot, also known as a darning foot, is a foot that hovers slightly above the surface of the fabric, allowing you to move the fabric in all directions as you stitch. Free-motion feet come in both open- and closed-toe varieties. The open toe allows for more visibility while you stitch, while a closed-toe foot is better to

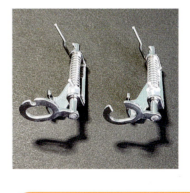

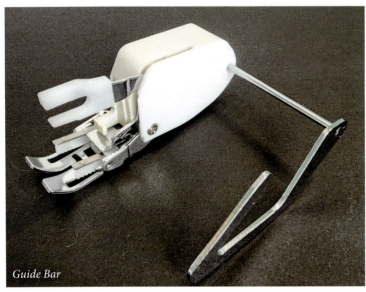

Guide Bar

Hack!

Sewing pedal moving on hardwood or tile floor? Use a couple rubber bands to make it nonslip. A silicone mat under the foot pedal can also make it nonslip.

use on bulkier fabrics or a fabric that has any kind of texture that could catch on the foot.

Cording Foot

A cording foot is used when adding embellishments like cord or yarn to a fabric. The foot has a narrow channel on the underside of the foot that holds the cord in place directly under the needle, making it easier to sew in place. Cording feet can have either one or multiple channels on the underside of the foot to accommodate multiple strands.

Piping Foot

A piping foot is used when making or attaching piping to a project. It has two wide channels on the underside of the foot that hold the piping in place when sewing. You

can use either channel to hold the piping in place when you stitch, depending on your needle position.

Pintuck Foot

A pintuck foot, used in conjunction with a twin needle, is used to sew pintucks into fabric. The foot has multiple narrow grooves on the underside. As the twin needle creates the pintucks while you sew, you can then move the pintuck to the next groove over to sew another row of pintucks,

keeping everything straight and aligned. Pintuck feet can come with different amounts of grooves on the underside.

Overcast Foot

An overcast foot is used when sewing over the edge of a fabric to keep it from fraying or raveling. It has a thin bar in the center of the foot that the needle passes back and forth over as you sew. This bar holds the edge of the fabric flat and prevents the thread from being pulled too tight around the edge and puckering it.

Blind-Hem Foot

A blind-hem foot, used in conjunction with a blind-hem stitch and the proper blind-hem folding technique (see page 159 for how to sew a blind hem), is used to sew blind hems on garments like

trousers and dress pants. The foot has a guide in the center that follows the fold of the fabric. When the zigzag stitch of the blind-hem stitch happens, the needle passes over the guide in the center, keeping the thread from being pulled too tight. The resulting stitch is very tiny and nearly invisible on the right side of the fabric. Blind-hem feet are generally adjustable.

Teflon Foot

A Teflon foot is a standard style presser foot made from Teflon. It is a non-stick surface,

> ### Hack!
> If you don't have a plastic or Teflon presser foot and you're trying to sew on vinyl, faux leather, or another fabric that tends to stick to the bottom of the presser foot, place a piece of tape on the bottom of the foot. Be sure to cut a small hole in the foot opening for the needle!

making it great to use when sewing with fabric like vinyl, faux leather, suede, or any other fabric that tends to stick to the bottom of the foot.

Zipper Foot

A zipper foot is used when sewing zippers into projects. The foot allows you to sew very close to the zipper teeth. Most zipper feet are adjustable or can be attached to the machine in two positions, allowing you to sew on either side of the zipper.

Rolled-Hem Foot

A rolled-hem foot is used for sewing a narrow or rolled hem along the edge of a fabric. It has a curved guide that rolls the fabric as you stitch, creating the hem. Rolled-hem feet can come in a variety of widths, allowing you to sew very narrow and slightly wider rolled hems. These feet work best on light- to medium-weight fabric.

Zipper Foot

Button Foot

A button foot is a small foot that can hold buttons in place as you sew them on by machine. It has a wide opening in the center, which allows you to easily see the holes of the button. Many button feet have a rubber grip on the bottom of the foot, which helps prevent the button from moving while under the foot.

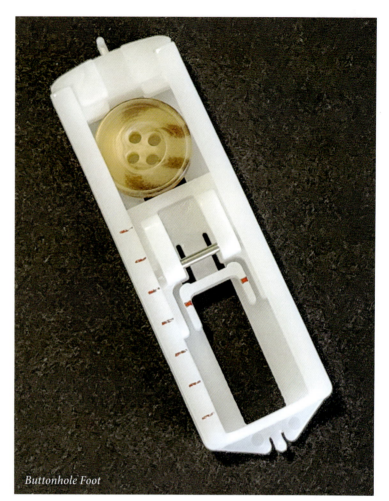

Buttonhole Foot

Buttonhole Foot

A buttonhole foot is a foot that helps you sew buttonholes onto projects. There are two main types of buttonhole feet: automatic and four-step. An automatic buttonhole foot has a space at the back of the foot that holds the button, which determines how long the buttonhole will be, and the machine can then stitch the buttonhole in one step.

A four-step buttonhole foot requires you to manually change the stitches between the top, bottom, and sides of the buttonhole as you stitch.

Roller Foot

A roller foot is a presser foot that has a small, texturized roller in the center of the foot that is designed to help feed "stickier" or textured fabrics through the machine. A roller foot can help prevent those fabrics from bunching or slipping while you sew.

Tip!

Presser feet can have different markings that are helpful when sewing. Lines that are parallel to the side of the foot can indicate different seam allowances. For example, if you want to topstitch ⅛" (3.2mm) away from the edge, use a foot with a mark ⅛" (3.2mm) away from the center of the foot. Lines that are perpendicular to the side of the foot can indicate how far away you are from the fabric edge. For example, if you are sewing with a ¼" (6.4mm) seam allowance and you want to stop ¼" (6.4mm) from the fabric edge so that you can pivot and start sewing down the next side, you would stop when the edge of the fabric is at the mark that is ¼" (6.4mm) from the center of the foot.

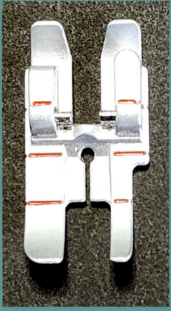

Techniques

Construction 36
Pockets 50
Sleeves 70
Cuffs 80
Collars 86
Elastic 92
Stabilizers and Interfacing 96
Seams 100
Other Ways to Embellish Fabric 106

Construction

Constructing your garment includes mastering techniques in stitching pockets, sleeves, cuffs, and more. Other construction techniques not only add shape and detail to projects, but can also impact a garments fit and finish.

Box Corners: Stitch Across Seams

Boxing corners is a great way to add a bottom to a bag or pouch without having to sew it in as a separate piece; you simply have a front and a back.

1. Sew the front and back pieces of your project together along the sides and lower edge, pivoting at the corners.

2. Starting on one side, align the side seam with the bottom seam and pin in place.

3. Determine how wide you want the bottom of the project to be. Divide that number in half, then measure and draw a line that distance away from the corner of the seam. For example; if you want the bottom of the project to be 2" (5.1cm), measure and draw a line 1" (2.5cm) away from the corner of the seam.

4. Stitch on the drawn line, then trim away the corner at the desired seam allowance.

5. Repeat on the other side, then turn right side out.

Hack!

A washer can be used when tracing a pattern piece to automatically add seam allowance as you go! The width of the washer from the center to the edge determines the seam allowance. Plus, no matter how the washer might rotate as you trace, the seam allowance stays the same.

Techniques / Construction

Box Corners: Cut Out Square

Another way to create a boxed corner on a project is to cut a square of fabric from the corner, and then sew the raw edges together.

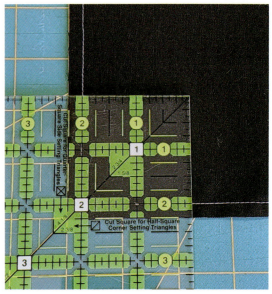

1. Start by sewing the sides and lower edge of the project together. Next, to determine the size of square to cut from your project, first decide how wide you want the bottom to be. Then, subtract double the seam allowance width and divide the number by 2. For example, if you are constructing a project using ¼" (6.4mm) seam allowances and you want the bottom of the project to measure 4 ½" (11.4cm), you would subtract ½" (1.2cm) from 4 ½" (11.4cm), then divide by 2, which equals 2, meaning you would cut a 2" (5.1cm) square from the corners of your project. Be sure to align the 2" (5.1cm) line of your ruler with the stitching line while cutting, not the raw edge of the fabric.

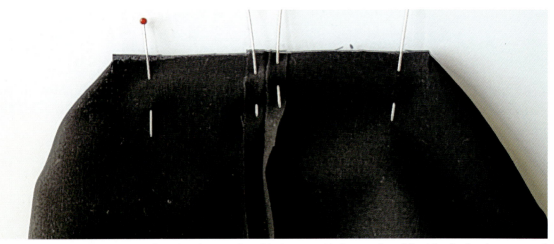

2. Press the seam allowances open, then align the raw edge of the bottom with the raw edge of the side, aligning the seams, and pin in place.

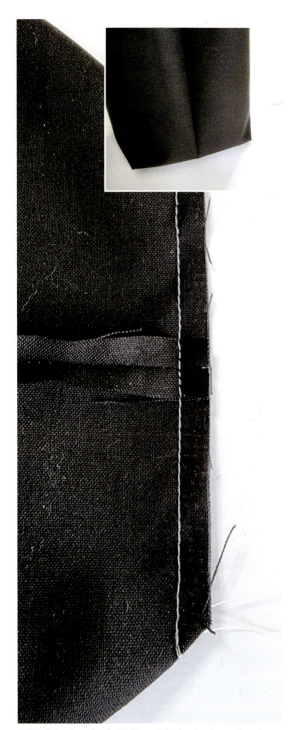

Hack!

If you find that the edge of a knit fabric keeps rolling while you stitch, making it hard to maintain the fabric edge along a seam allowance line, use a seam allowance magnet to keep the fabric lying flat. Make sure the gap between the magnet and the machine bed is high enough to accommodate your fabric—you want it to keep it from curling, but not stretch it while you sew!

3. Stitch in place, backstitching at the beginning and end. Turn right side out and press.

Godet

A godet, also known as a gore, is an extra section of fabric generally cut in a triangular shape, with either a straight or curved lower edge that is inserted into a garment to add volume or extra width, like along the lower edge of a skirt.

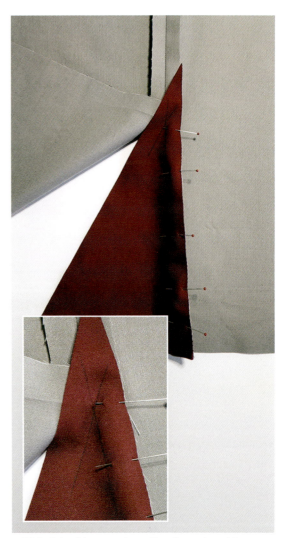

1. To sew a godet, start by sewing the remainder of the seam that will be above the godet in a garment using a ⅝" (1.6cm) seam allowance.

2. On the wrong side of the godet, mark the seam allowances on both sides near the point. This will create an X on the fabric.

3. With right sides together, align the godet with one side of the seam opening of the garment, aligning the lower edges. The X on the wrong side of the godet should be directly above the lower edge of the sewn seam.

4. Sew the side of the godet to the garment, starting at the lower edge and ending at the X. Backstitch at the beginning and end of the stitching.

5. Repeat to attach the other side of the godet to the other side of the garment opening, then press the seam allowances toward the garment.

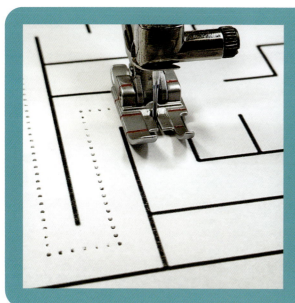

Tip!

If you are just learning to sew, or want to practice sewing straight lines or curves, use a maze! With no thread in the machine, sew your way through a maze printed on standard printer paper. This can help you practice maintaining a consistent seam allowance by staying in the center of the lines, while also allowing you to practice curves and pivoting at corners.

Easy Skirt Slit

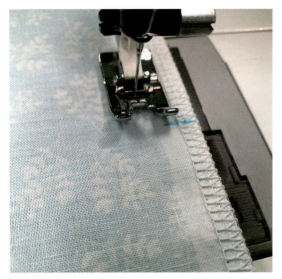 

1. Along the side or back seam where the slit is being added, finish the fabric edge, and then hem the skirt. From the lower hemmed edge, measure up and mark 4" (10.2cm). With right sides together, sew from the upper edge of the skirt to the mark.

2. Cut a 10" (25.4cm) piece of ⅝" (1.6cm) wide twill tape. Place the center of the tape at the mark, perpendicular to the fabric edge. Using a ⅝" (1.6cm) seam allowance, stitch over the tape twice to secure it in place.

3. Trim across the seam allowance, just below the twill tape.

4. Fold the left side of the seam allowance to the left. Fold the right side of the twill tape down over itself at a 45° angle. The outer edge of the tape will align with the outer edge of the seam allowance.

5. Stitch the twill tape in place approximately ⅛" (3.2mm) from the inner edge.

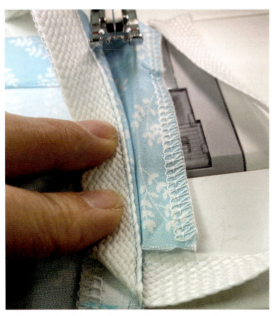

6. Rotate the skirt so that the lower hemmed edge is closest to the needle. Hold the stitched side of the seam allowance to the left, and open the remaining seam allowance so that it lays flat.

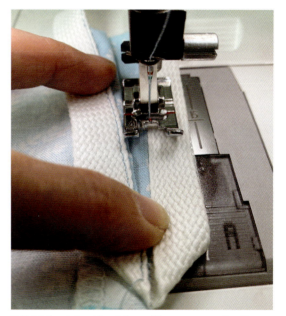

7. Fold the right side of the twill tape up over itself at a 45° angle, align the outer edges of the tape and fabric, and then stitch in place ⅛" (3.2mm) from the inner edge of the tape.

8. Trim off the excess twill tape ¾" (2cm) from the lower hemmed edge.

9. Fold the end of the twill tape under until the fold aligns with the lower edge of the skirt.

10. Starting at the folded edge, stitch the twill tape in place ⅛" (3.2mm) from the edge. Stop with the needle down at the corners to pivot and continue stitching.

11. Fold under the remaining twill tape end until the folded edge aligns with the lower edge of the skirt, then stitch the remaining tape in place.

12. If desired, secure the top of the slit with a triangle of stitching.

Techniques / Construction **45**

Easy Pant Slit

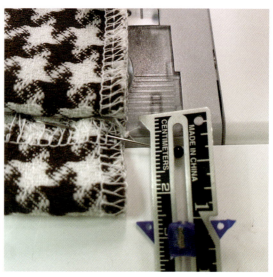

1. Finish the fabric edges with a zigzag or overcast stitch. Along the side seam, measure and mark 2" (5.1cm) from the lower edge. Using a ⅝" (1.6cm) seam allowance, and with the fabric right sides together, stitch the side seam from the upper edge to the mark.

2. Fold the top layer of fabric up out of the way and secure with a pin. With right sides together, fold the lower layer of fabric up 1" (2.5cm) and pin in place.

3. Using a ⅝" (1.6cm) seam allowance, stitch the fold in place.

4. Remove the pin holding the top layer of fabric out of the way, then rotate the pant leg so that layer of fabric is closest to the needle. Hold the previously stitched fold out of the way, then with right sides together, fold the remaining fabric raw edge down 1" (2.5cm).

5. Starting at the fold and using a ⅝" (1.6cm) seam allowance, stitch the fold in place.

6. Turn the folds right side out and press.

Techniques / Construction **47**

Gusset

A gusset is an extra section of fabric, generally cut in a triangular or diamond shape, that is inserted into a garment to add extra space and reduce potential stress on a seam, like in the crotch or underarm area of a garment. For this example, a gusset will be added to a pair of pants.

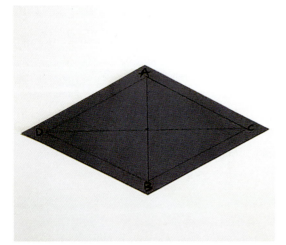

1. Start by determining the amount of extra fabric that needs to be added to the garment. The easiest way to do this is to unpick the seams along the center crotch seam and several inches along both inseams. With the pants on, measure the gap in the crotch between the front and back. For this example, 2 ½" (6.4cm) will be used. Gussets are typically made from fabric that matches the garment, but a contrasting fabric will be shown here.

2. Pant gussets are generally diamond in shape, and the length of the gusset is at least twice the width, meaning the gusset in this example would be 5" (12.7cm) long. Draw a diamond shape that is 2 ½" (6.4cm) wide and 5" (12.7cm) long, and then add seam allowance width around the perimeter of the diamond. For this example, ¼" (6.4mm) will be used. The points have been labeled A, B, C, and D for alignment reference in the next step.

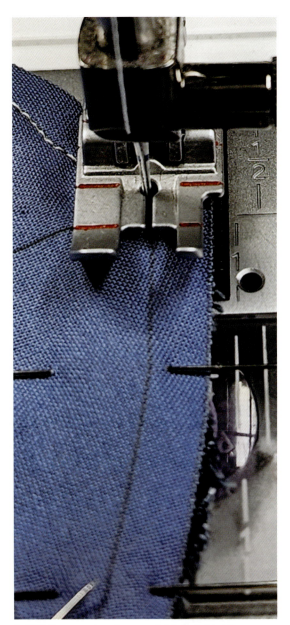

Hack!

Tape two pencils together to quickly and easily draw both a pattern line and the seam allowance line at the same time.

4. Sew along the drawn seam allowance lines, stopping at the points with the needle down and pivoting the fabric to align with the next side to be stitched. Overlap the stitching end and beginning.

3. With the gusset and garment fabric right sides together, start by aligning point A with the center front crotch seam and pin in place. Align point B with the center back crotch seam and pin in place. Align points C and D with the inseams on either side and pin in place. Note that, depending on how much of the inseam you originally unpicked, there may still be some unstitched past the end of the gusset. That can be restitched later.

Techniques / Construction

Pockets

No matter the garment—is there anything better than pockets? Whether you are adding them to the front of shirts and jackets or the side seams of pants, skirts, or dresses, there's a pocket for every garment.

Angled Patch Pocket

An angled patch pocket is a pocket commonly found on the front of dress shirts.

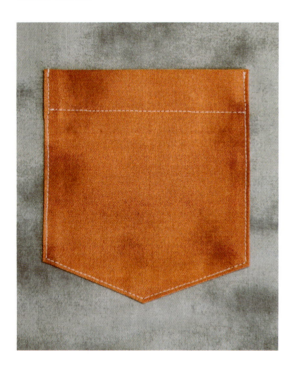

1. To sew an angled patch pocket, start by finishing the sides and lower edges of the pocket with a zigzag or overcast stitch. Then, fold the upper pocket edge ¼" (6.4mm) toward the wrong side and press in place.

> **Tip!**
> If you don't want to see the line of stitching on the top of the pocket, secure the fold in place with fusible hem tape.

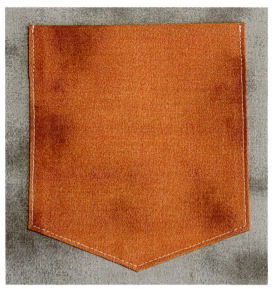

2. Along the sides and lower edges, fold the fabric ¼" (6.4mm) toward the wrong side and press. Then, fold the upper edge toward the wrong side along the fold line indicated on the pocket pattern piece, or approximately ¾" (1.9cm) from the upper edge and press. Stitch the upper fold in place close to the lower edge.

> **Tip!**
> If you find that the edges aren't staying pressed flat after you remove the iron, flip the fabric over and press the fold in place from the right side. After you remove the iron from the fabric, let the fabric cool before picking it up and moving on to the next step.

3. Place the pocket on the shirt front where indicated on the pattern, and then stitch in place along the sides and lower edge approximately ⅛" (3.2mm) from the edge. Start the stitching at the upper edge of the pocket on one side and end the stitching at the upper edge on the other side of the pocket, backstitching at the beginning and end, and pivoting at the corners.

> **Tip!**
> If you're sewing lots of little pieces together, don't cut the threads after each piece. Use a technique called chain piecing, where you simply sew off the end of one piece right onto the next. This leaves a small "chain" of thread between each piece that can be cut to separate the pieces. If you are sewing something that needs backstitching at the beginning and end, you can still use this technique.

Techniques / Pockets

Rounded Patch Pocket

A rounded patch pocket is created essentially the same way as an angled patch pocket, except that the lower edges are rounded.

1. Finish the edges of the pocket and prepare the first upper fold the same way as the angled patch pocket.

3. With the cardstock template centered on the wrong wide of the pocket fabric, press the fabric edges ¼" (6.4mm) toward the wrong side along the edge of the cardstock. Then, fold the upper edge toward the wrong side along the fold line indicated on the pocket pattern piece, or approximately ¾" (1.9cm) from the upper edge and press.

2. When pressing the sides and lower edges of a rounded patch pocket, it can be helpful to use a template. From a piece of cardstock or template plastic, cut out the rounded patch pocket pattern piece, then trim ¼" (6.4mm) from the sides and lower edge.

4. Place the pocket on the shirt front as desired or where indicated on the pattern, and then stitch in place along the sides and lower edge approximately ⅛" (3.2mm) from the edge. Start the stitching at the upper edge of the pocket on one side and end the stitching at the upper edge on the other side of the pocket, backstitching at the beginning and end.

Tip!

If you don't have cardstock, run a line of basting stitches ¼" (6.4mm) from the edge of the fabric and use the stitching line as a guide for where to fold. Once the fold has been pressed in place, the basting stitches can be removed.

Utility Pocket

A utility pocket, or pencil pocket, is a patch pocket with either angled or rounded lower edges that has an extra line of stitching along one side that serves as pencil holder. Once the pocket has been stitched to the shirt, sew an additional line of stitching approximately ¾" (1.9cm) from one edge, backstitching at the beginning and end.

Hack!

If you're cutting around the edge of a pattern and want to add in a seam allowance as you cut, place several magnets that measure the seam allowance width on the end of your scissors. Be sure to place them on the top blade far enough up the scissors that they don't keep the blades from completely closing. Align the end of the magnets with the pattern piece and cut the fabric with the added seam allowance!

Pocket Dog Ears

Pocket dog ears are small triangles of stitching that are added to the upper corners of a pocket to reinforce it.

Techniques / Pockets

Patch Pocket with Piping Border

Patch pockets with either angled or rounded lower edges can even be embellished with piping! Start by making a patch pocket, then measure the total length of the sides and lower edges. Prepare a length of piping that is ½" (1.2cm) longer than the total length. (See page 197 for how to make piping.) Finish the piping ends, then align it with the folded edge of the pocket and pin in place. Place the pocket on the shirt front as desired, or where indicated on the pattern, and then stitch in place along the sides and lower edge approximately 1/16" (1.6mm) from the edge. Start the stitching at the upper edge of the pocket on one side and end the stitching at the upper edge on the other side of the pocket, backstitching at the beginning and end.

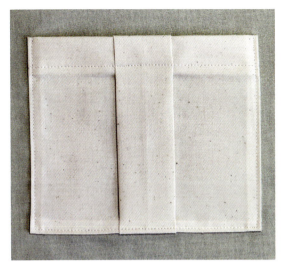

Safari Pocket

A safari pocket is a patch-style pocket with a box pleat in the center. It can be added to the front of shirts and jackets or even added as back pockets on pants. Safari pockets can be made with or without a pocket flap at the top.

1. Safari pockets can be made in a variety of sizes, but for this example, a 10" x 7" (25.4cm x 17.8cm) rectangle will be used. Fold the rectangle in half with wrong sides together, then sew a line of stitching 1 ½" (1.2cm) away from the folded edge.

2. Open the fabric, lay it flat on a surface with the right side up, then align the center fold of the rectangle over the stitching line.

3. Press the pocket flat, then finish the sides and lower edge with a zigzag or overcast stitch.

4. Along the upper edge, fold the fabric ¼" (6.4mm) toward the wrong side and press. Fold the upper edge again ¾" (1.9cm) toward the wrong side and press, then stitch in place close to the lower folded edge. Fold the sides and lower edge ¼" (6.4mm) toward the wrong side and press.

5. Place the pocket on the garment where desired, and then stitch in place along the sides and lower edge approximately ⅛" (3.2mm) from the edge. Start the stitching at the upper edge of the pocket on one side and end the stitching at the upper edge on the other side of the pocket, backstitching at the beginning and end.

Inverted Box Pleat Pocket

An inverted or reverse pleat pocket is a patch pocket with an inverted box pleat folded into the center. These pockets are commonly found on the front of shirts and jackets, but they can also be used on pants. Inverted box pleat pockets can be made with or without a pocket flap at the top.

> ### Tip!
> If you don't have a removable fabric marker handy, use a hera marker to mark the line along the center of the fabric, and make small marks with a standard pencil along the edge where they will be hidden in a seam allowance.

1. These pockets can be made in a variety of sizes, but for this example, a 9" x 7" (22.9cm x 17.8cm) rectangle will be used. Using a removable fabric marker, mark the center of the rectangle on the right side of the fabric, then mark a line 1" (2.5cm) on the left and 1" (2.5cm) on the right. Make the marks on both the top and bottom of the rectangle.

> ### Tip!
> Add bar tacks to areas of garments that undergo heavy wear and tear or stress, like the upper edges of pockets, the lower edge of a pant fly opening, or even belt loops. To sew a bar tack, shorten your stitch length by half to approximately 1mm and sew a short line of stitches. Backstitch over all the stitches, then sew forward over them one more time to secure.

2. Fold the fabric to bring the 1" (2.5cm) marks on right to the center of the rectangle and press. Repeat to bring the 1" (2.5cm) marks on the left to the center of the rectangle and press, then finish the sides and lower edges of the pocket with a zigzag or overcast stitch.

3. Along the upper edge, fold the fabric ¼" (6.4mm) toward the wrong side and press. Fold the upper edge again ¾" (1.9cm) toward the wrong side and press, then stitch in place close to the lower folded edge. Place the pocket on the garment where desired, and then stitch in place along the sides and lower edge approximately ⅛" (3.2mm) from the edge. Start the stitching at the upper edge of the pocket on one side and end the stitching at the upper edge on the other side of the pocket, backstitching at the beginning and end.

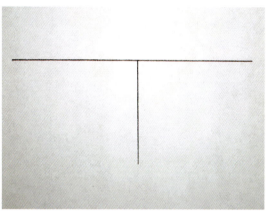

Rounded Pocket Flaps

Pocket flaps can be added to the top of nearly any kind of pocket. They can be made with either an angled or rounded lower edge and are sometimes made to either match or complement the pocket style.

1. To make a pocket flap pattern piece, start by measuring the width of the pocket that the flap is going over. The pocket flap pattern piece needs to be ½" (1.2cm) wider than the pocket. For this example, 6½" (16.5cm) will be used. The center depth of a pocket flap is generally around ⅓ the height of the pocket. For this example, 3" (7.6cm) will be used. Draw the 6½" (16.5cm) line horizontally first, then draw the 3" (7.6cm) line perpendicularly in the center.

2. Connect the ends of the horizontal line in the center using a curved line, then cut out the pattern piece.

Techniques / Pockets

Tip!

Draw the desired curve on one half of the pocket flap first, then cut it out. Fold the pocket flap in half, and then trace the curve onto the other side. This will ensure that both curves are identical.

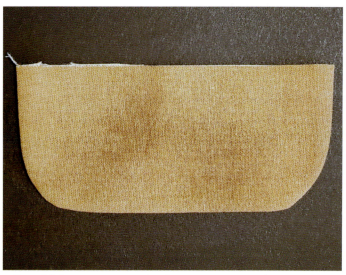

3. From fabric, cut out two pocket flap pattern pieces. Align the pieces with right sides together and stitch along the curved edge using a ¼" (6.4mm) seam allowance. Trim the seam allowance by approximately half, then turn the pocket flap right side out and press.

4. Place the pocket flap slightly above the upper edge of the pocket, then stitch in place ¼" (6.4mm) from the raw edge.

5. Trim the raw edge of the pocket flap by approximately half.

6. Fold the pocket flap down over the pocket along the previous stitching line, then stitch in place ¼" (6.4mm) from the upper edge, backstitching at the beginning and end.

Angled Pocket Flap

Pocket flaps with angled lower edges are constructed and attached the same way. Both rounded and angled pocket flaps can be secured with button closures. If you are adding a button closure to a pocket flap, sew a buttonhole onto the center of the pocket flap approximately ½" (1.2cm) from the lower edge before attaching the flap to the shirt. Then, after attaching the flap, position a button on the pocket underneath the buttonhole and hand stitch in place.

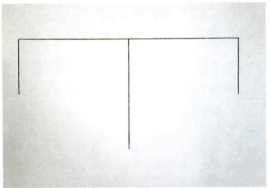

1. To make a pocket flap with an angled lower edge, again start by measuring the width of the pocket the flap is going over. The pocket flap pattern piece needs to be ½" (1.2cm) wider than the pocket. For this example, 6½" (16.5cm) will be used. The center depth of a pocket flap is generally around ⅓ the height of the pocket. For this example, 3" (7.6cm) will be used. Draw the 6½" (16.5cm) line horizontally first, then draw the 3" (7.6cm) line perpendicularly in the center. Next, at both ends of the line, draw a 1½" (3.8cm) perpendicular line.

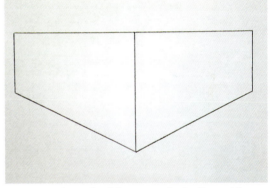

2. Connect the ends of the perpendicular lines with two angled lines toward the lower center. These lines can be drawn freehand or by using a curved ruler.

3. Cut out, construct, and attach just like a rounded pocket flap.

Trick!

When sewing on a button, hide both the starting and ending knots under the button!

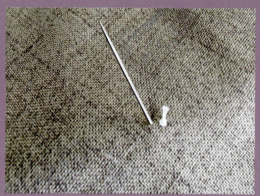

1. Take a length of thread with a knot at the end through the fabric from the right side at the desired button location, and then bring the thread back up though the fabric close to the knot.

2. Take the needle and thread up through one of the openings in the button, then back down through the other opening and through the fabric.

3. Repeat to take several stitches through the button openings to secure, then bring the needle up though the fabric under the button and pull to the side.

4. Wrap the thread around the button and pull until there is a small loop of thread. Insert the needle into the thread loop.

5. Pull the thread tight and repeat two or three times to secure and clip the thread. There will only be a small stitch visible on the other side of the fabric.

Tip!

Place a toothpick as a spacer under the button when you stitch to ensure you have enough space between the button and fabric when a garment is buttoned.

Western Pocket Flap

A Western pocket flap is another common pocket flap on both men's and women's shirts. Rather than being secured with a button, this pocket flap style is generally secured with a pearl snap.

> **Tip!**
> When cutting out pattern pieces, keep your scissors between you and the pattern piece—meaning not reaching across the pattern to cut at the farthest away edge. This will give you the most accuracy when cutting out pieces.

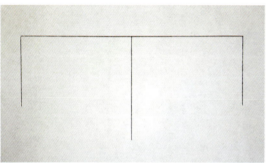
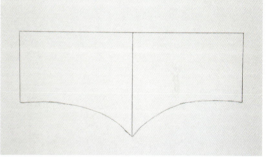

1. To make a Western pocket flap with an angled lower edge, again start by measuring the width of the pocket the flap is going over. The pocket flap pattern piece needs to be ½" (1.2cm) wider than the pocket. For this example, 6 ½" (16.5cm) will be used. The center depth of a pocket flap is generally around ⅓ the height of the pocket. For this example, 3" (7.6cm) will be used. Draw the 6 ½" (16.5cm) line horizontally first, then draw the 3" (7.6cm) line perpendicularly in the center. Next, at both ends of the line, draw a 2" (5.1cm) perpendicular line.

2. Connect the ends of the perpendicular line with two curved lines toward the lower center. These lines can be drawn freehand or by using a curved ruler.

3. Cut out, construct, and attach just like a rounded pocket flap.

Welt Pocket

A welt pocket is a garment pocket where the opening is framed with a narrow strip of fabric, or a welt. Welt pockets are commonly found on trousers, jackets, and tailored coats.

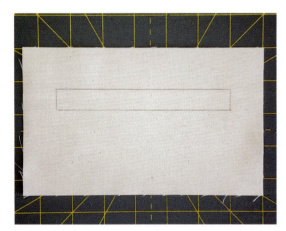
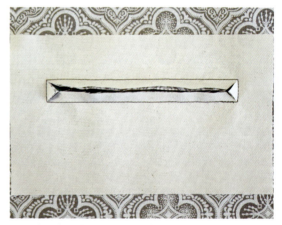

1. To make a welt pocket, start by cutting a rectangle of fabric that will become the welt strip. For this example, the welt rectangle is cut at 4½" x 7½" (11.4cm x 19.1cm). If you are using a lighter-weight fabric, apply fusible interfacing to the wrong side of the fabric. Approximately ⅓ of the way down the rectangle from the upper edge, center and draw a ⅝" x 5½" (1.6cm x 14cm) rectangle.

2. With right sides together, place the welt rectangle on the garment where you want the pocket opening to be. Stitch in place along the long lines of the rectangle. Then, starting and stopping approximately ½" (1.2cm) from the short ends, cut a line along the center of the rectangle, then cut short, angled clips toward the corners.

3. Push the entire piece of welt rectangle fabric through the cut opening, toward the wrong side, and then press flat.

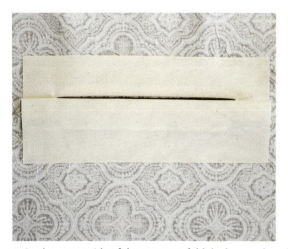

4. On the wrong side of the garment, fold the lower edge of the welt rectangle up over the rectangle opening, then back down until the upper folded edge is at the upper edge of the opening. Press in place.

5. On the right side, fold one side of the garment fabric back to reveal the edges of the welt rectangle and a small triangle of the garment fabric. Stitch in place close to the fold of the garment fabric. Then, repeat on the other side.

6. From the same fabric as the garment, cut a facing rectangle. This rectangle will be directly behind the pocket opening and will prevent the pocket-lining fabric from being seen. For this example, the rectangle will be cut at 4" x 7½" (10.2cm x 19.1cm). From a lining fabric, cut a pocket-lining rectangle that measures 7 ½" (19.1cm) wide by the desired pocket depth + ½" (1.2cm). For this example, the rectangle will be cut at 7½" x 5½" (19.1cm x 14cm) and be referred to as Pocket Lining A. Also from the lining fabric, cut a long pocket-lining rectangle that measures 7½" x 4¼" (19.1cm x 10.8cm). This rectangle will be referred to as Pocket Lining B.

7. With right sides together, sew the facing rectangle to Pocket Lining B using a ¼" (6.4mm) seam allowance, and then finish the seam using a zigzag or overcast stitch.

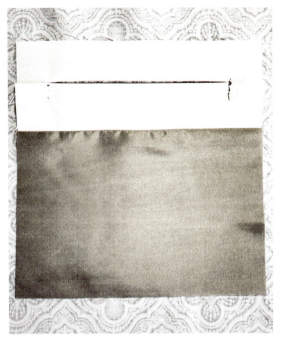

8. With right sides together, sew Pocket Lining A to the lower edge of the welt fabric using only a ½" (1.2cm) seam allowance, and then press the fabric and seam allowances down, away from the pocket opening.

9. With right sides together, sew the facing rectangle to the upper edge of the welt fabric using only a ¼" (6.4mm) seam allowance, and then finish the seam using a zigzag or overcast stitch.

10. Align the sides of Pocket Lining A with the sides of Pocket Lining B and facing, and stitch using a ⅝" (1.6cm) seam allowance. Trim the seam allowance by approximately half, and then finish the seam using a zigzag or overcast stitch.

Inseam Pocket

An inseam pocket is a pocket sewn into the seam of a garment. They are generally found on the side seams of pants or dresses.

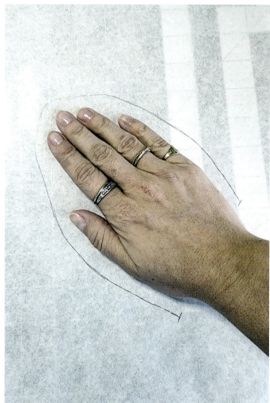

1. To sew an inseam pocket, start by cutting two pocket bag pattern pieces. If you are not following a pattern, you can draft your own pattern piece by laying your hand on a piece of pattern drafting paper and roughly tracing around it to get the desired pocket size. Note that you will be losing ⅝" (1.6cm) around the perimeter of the pocket as it is assembled, so if you want a roomy pocket, make sure you leave space between your hand and the drawn lines. Mark where your wrist is so that you know how long to make the pocket opening.

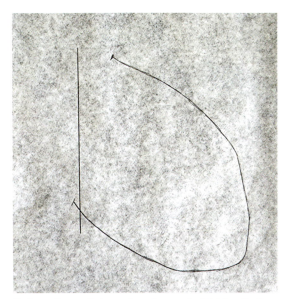

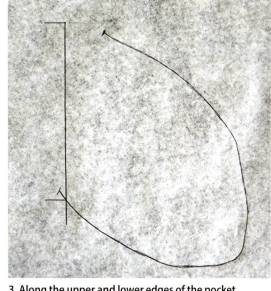

2. Along the pocket opening, draw a straight line that is somewhat parallel to the opposite side of the pocket bag. Note that this line will not align exactly with the upper and lower lines of the pocket opening. These will be adjusted later.

3. Along the upper and lower edges of the pocket opening line, draw a ⅝" (1.6cm) perpendicular line away from the pocket.

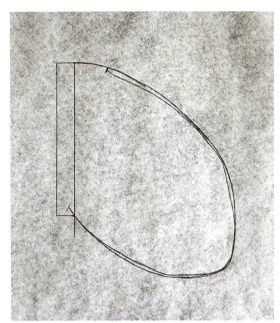

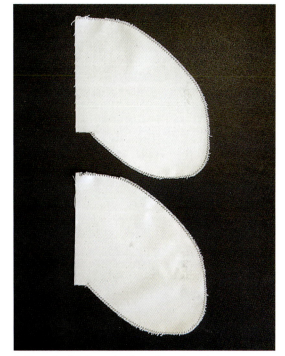

4. Draw a new line along the pocket opening, connect the pocket bag lines to the ends of the perpendicular lines, and then true up or smooth out the pattern lines.

5. Once the fabric pocket bag pieces have been cut, finish the curved edges of the pocket bag pieces using a zigzag or overcast stitch.

6. With right sides together, pin one pocket bag piece to the front of the garment at the desired pocket placement, and then stitch in place using a ⅝" (1.6cm) seam allowance.

7. Repeat to attach the remaining pocket bag piece to the back of the garment, ensuring that it is the same distance from the upper edge as the pocket bag attached to the garment front. Press the pocket bags away from the garment front and back, and then topstitch approximately ⅛" (3.2mm) from the seam.

9. Starting at the garment's upper edge, sew the side seam and pocket bag using a ⅝" (1.6cm) seam allowance.

10. Press the pocket toward the garment front.

8. Align the garment front and back, ensuring that the garment side seams as well as the pocket bags are aligned, and then pin in place.

Techniques / Pockets

Sleeves

Sleeves can be an intimidating part of a garment. However, if you cut your pattern pieces accurately, align the proper notches and marks, and use one of the following insertion methods, you'll be adding sleeves to garments with ease in no time.

Set-In Sleeve

A set-in sleeve is a sleeve that is sewn into a garment after both the shoulder and side seams have been stitched.

1. Cut out the front, back, and sleeve pieces of the garment and transfer all notches and marks. Then, sew the shoulder and side seams of the garment and finish the seam allowances as desired.

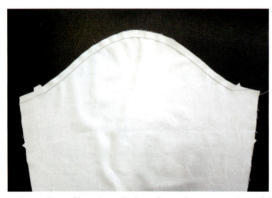

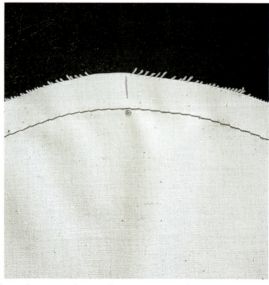

2. Sew a line of basting stitches along the upper edge of the sleeve between the notches approximately ½" (1.2cm) from the raw edge.

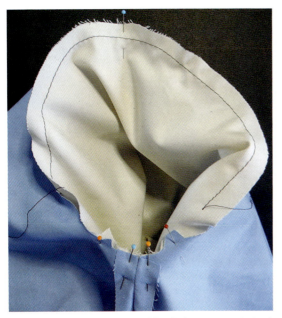

3. Sew the underarm seam and finish the seam as desired. Then, with right sides together, align the double notch of the sleeve with the double notch on the back of the garment. Align the single notch of the sleeve with the single notch on the front of the garment, and align the underarm seam with the side seam of the garment. Align the mark along the upper curved edge of the sleeve with the shoulder seam and pin all in place. It is easiest to do this with the shirt inside out and the sleeve right side out.

4. Along the upper edge of the sleeve, pull on the bobbin thread of the basting stitches to slightly gather the fabric and help evenly distribute the sleeve fabric over the remainder of the armhole opening. Pin in place roughly every 1" (2.5cm). Be sure not to intentionally pin any fabric puckers in place.

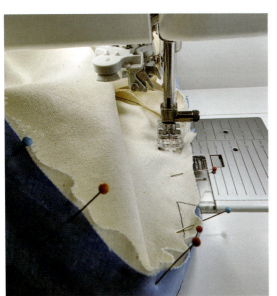

5. With the sleeve fabric on top, stitch the sleeve in place using a ⅝" (1.6 cm) seam allowance. Having the sleeve fabric on top will allow you to see any potential puckers in the sleeve fabric and adjust the fabric as you sew if needed.

6. Remove the basting stitches and finish the seam allowance as desired.

Tip!

It can seem like a lot of fabric bunched up around the needle as you sew, but only focus on the fabric directly under the needle—it's the only fabric that needs to be lying flat.

Flat Sleeve Insertion

If you find sewing set-in sleeves to be difficult, another option is to sew the sleeve to the front and back of the garment while they are still lying flat.

 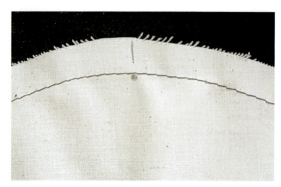

1. Start by cutting out the front, back, and sleeve pieces of the garment and transferring all notches and marks. Then, sew the front and back pieces together at the shoulder seam only and finish the seam allowance as desired. Next, sew a line of basting stitches along the upper edge of the sleeve between the notches approximately ½" (1.2cm) from the raw edge.

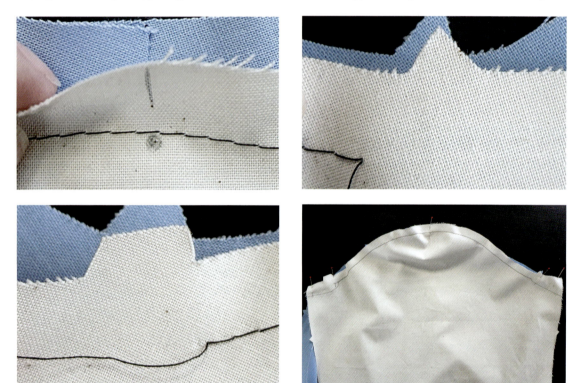

2. With right sides together, align the mark along the upper curved edge of the sleeve with the shoulder seam and pin in place. Then, align the double notch of the sleeve with the double notch on the back of the garment. Align the single notch of the sleeve with the single notch on the front of the garment, and the edges of the sleeve with the edge of the front and back. Pin all in place.

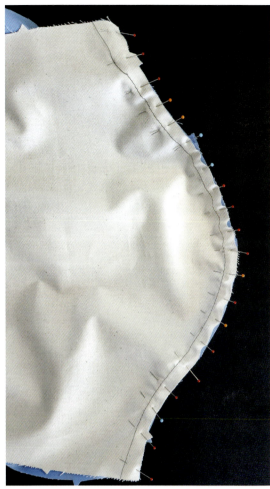

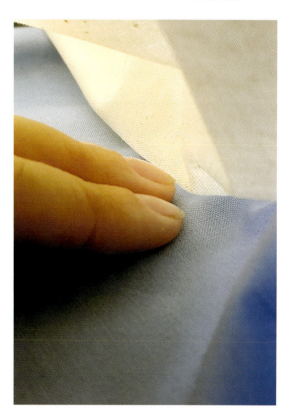

4. With the sleeve fabric on top, stitch the sleeve in place using a ⅝" (1.6cm) seam allowance. Remove the basting stitches and finish the seam allowance as desired. Then, sew the underarm and side seam using a ⅝" (1.6cm) seam allowance and finish the seam allowances as well.

3. Along the upper edge of the sleeve, pull on the bobbin thread of the basting stitches to slightly gather the fabric and help evenly distribute the sleeve fabric over the remainder of the armhole opening. Pin in place roughly every 1" (2.5cm). Be sure not to intentionally pin any fabric puckers in place.

Tip!

When sewing the sleeve seam, place your left hand between the fabric layers with your fingers just to the left of the presser foot. This will help you feel for puckers that might appear in the shirt fabric that you can't see through the sleeve fabric, and help you make necessary adjustments while stitching.

Sleeve Placket

On most button-down shirts, whether they are men's or women's, it is common for the shirt to have a placket at the lower edge of the sleeve. This allows the sleeve and cuff to open further and make the sleeve easier to put on.

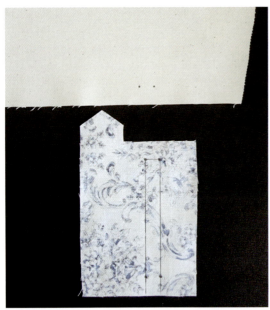

1. Cut out the sleeve and placket pieces. Transfer the markings from the placket pattern piece to the wrong side of the placket fabric, and the markings from the sleeve pattern piece to the wrong side of the sleeve fabric.

2. Along the upper point of the placket and the side nearest the point, fold and press the fabric ¼" (6.4mm) toward the wrong side.

3. Align the right side of the placket fabric with the wrong side of the sleeve fabric at the marks. At this point, the pointed side of the placket should be closest to the notch along the lower edge.

4. With the placket fabric up, sew the long and short ends of the marked rectangle.

5. Starting at the lower edge, cut along the center of the stitched rectangle, stopping approximately ¼" (6.4mm) from the upper edge. Then, cut at a diagonal from the end of the previous cut to the corners.

6. Push the placket through the cut opening toward the right side of the fabric and press flat.

7. Working on the short side of the placket, fold and press the raw edge ¼" (6.4mm) toward the wrong side. Then, fold the short side until the pressed edge is just over the stitching line. Pin in place.

Techniques / Sleeves

8. Stitch the short side of the placket in place approximately 1/16" (1.6mm) from the folded edge.

9. Working on the pointed side of the placket, open the fabric to see the stitching line, then fold the placket in half until the pressed edge is just over the stitching line. Pin in place.

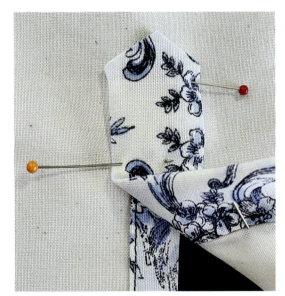

10. On the other side of the placket, place a pin to mark the top of the placket opening.

11. Starting at the sleeve edge and using a 1/8" (3.2mm) seam allowance, sew up the side of the placket to the upper point, pivot, and then sew down the other side of the placket to the pin at the top of the placket opening. Pivot again and sew across the top of the placket opening, then backstitch to secure. The sleeve is now ready to attach to a cuff!

Sleeve Placket with Fabric Strip

A simplified way to create a finished edge along a placket opening is to use a strip of fabric.

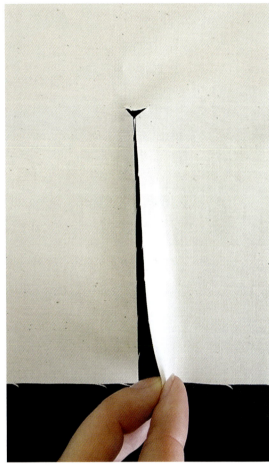

1. Cut out a sleeve pattern piece and cut along the placket opening indicated on the pattern piece. This should be one long straight cut with two short diagonal cuts at the upper edge.

2. Cut a 2 ½" (6.4cm) wide strip of fabric. Fold and press the long edges ¼" (6.4mm) toward the wrong side, then fold the strip in half with wrong sides together and press again.

3. Open the cut in the sleeve until it forms a straight line, folding the excess fabric toward the center. Open the pressed fabric strip, and slide it over the raw edge of the sleeve by approximately ¼" (6.4mm).

Techniques / Sleeves

4. Stitch the fabric strip in place approximately 1/16" (1.6mm) from the folded edge.

5. With the right side of the sleeve fabric up, fold the wide side of the sleeve away from the narrow side at a 90° angle. The tape will form a point at the upper edge of the opening.

6. Pinch the 45° fold in the fabric strip to hold it in place, and then fold the wide side of the sleeve down over the narrow side.

7. Sewing approximately 1/16" (1.6mm) from the edge, sew a small pentagon shape in the top of the fabric strip to secure the fold.

Techniques / Sleeves

Cuffs

Cuffs are the perfect finish to the lower edge of a sleeve. And, with several cuff types to choose from, you can completely change the look of a sleeve with each one.

Barrel Cuff

A barrel cuff is one of the more standard shirt cuffs and is essentially just a large rectangle that measures the length of the sleeve opening by the desired cuff width plus a seam allowance.

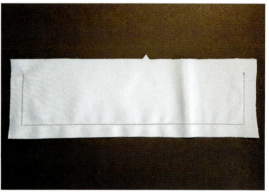

1. To sew a barrel cuff, place the two cuff rectangles right sides together and stitch the sides and lower edge using a ⅝" (1.6cm) seam allowance, starting and stopping the stitching ⅝" (1.6cm) from the upper edge.

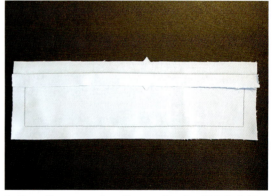

2. Along the upper edge of one rectangle of fabric, fold and press ⅝" (1.6cm) toward the wrong side.

3. Clip the corners, then turn the cuff right side out and press.

5. Press the seam allowances toward the cuff, then position the folded edge of the cuff over the previous stitching line and pin in place.

6. Topstitch the cuff in place approximately ⅛" (3.2mm) from the folded edge.

4. Sew the buttonhole on one side of the cuff as marked on a pattern. Then, with right sides together, align the unpressed edge of the cuff with the lower edge of the sleeve and stitch in place using a ⅝" (1.6cm) seam allowance. The buttonhole side of the cuff should align with the placket side of the sleeve.

Tip!

Always lengthen the stitch length when topstitching. This makes it easier to keep a straight line along the edge of a project, and it makes for a more professional look. A standard stitch length is between 2–2.5mm, meaning a topstitching length should be around 3–3.5mm.

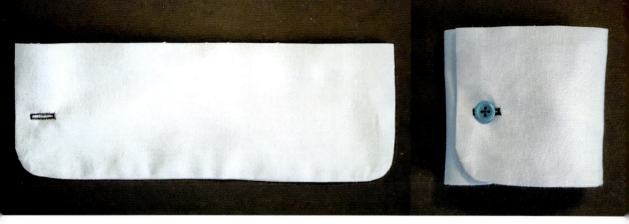

Rounded Cuff

A rounded cuff is just a barrel cuff with a rounded lower edge.

1. Cut out the cuff rectangle pattern piece. At the lower edge, measure and mark 1" (2.5cm) from the corner along the lower edge and side.

2. Using a circle template, a spool of thread, or anything similar in size, connect the marks on the corners of the rectangles with a curved line and then cut away the excess. Fold the cuff in half and trace the curved line on the other corner. This will ensure that the curves are identical.

3. Construct and attach the cuff like a standard barrel cuff.

Mitered Cuff

A mitered cuff is a barrel cuff with a 45° cut along the lower edge.

1. Cut out the cuff rectangle pattern piece. At the lower edge, measure and mark 1" (2.5cm) from the corner along the lower edge and side. Using a straight ruler, connect the marks on the corner of the rectangle, and then cut away the excess. Fold the cuff in half and trace the line on the other corner. This will ensure that the sides are identical.

2. Construct and attach the cuff like a standard barrel cuff.

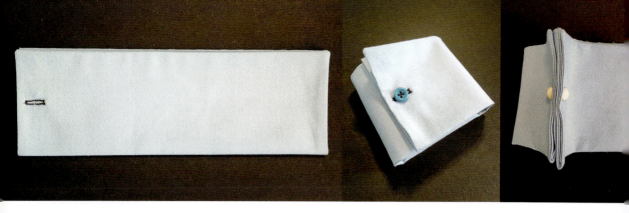

French Cuff

A French cuff is simply a cuff that is twice as wide as a standard barrel cuff. It is constructed and attached like a barrel cuff, then folded back on itself and secured using either buttons or cuff links. If you plan to use cufflinks rather than buttons, simply add buttonholes to both sides of the cuff.

Tip!

Want to create the look of a cuff link? Sew two shank buttons together. Have fun with your button selection! Just make sure at least one of the buttons can fit through the buttonholes.

Turnback Cuff

A turnback cuff, sometimes referred to as a cocktail cuff, is a variation of a French cuff. Similar to a French cuff, it is twice the width of a standard barrel cuff; however, it has a slight taper along the lower edge that allows the buttons to be visible when it is folded back.

1. Start by cutting a rectangle that is twice as wide as a barrel cuff. On one short side of the cuff, measure and mark the center, then measure in 2 ½" (6.4cm) from the side along the lower edge and mark.

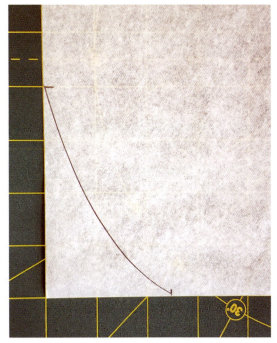

2. Connect the mark at the lower edge and the mark at the center with a gentle curve using a curved ruler, then cut away the excess.

3. Fold the cuff in half and trace the cut edge on the other side of the cuff, aligning the cut curve with the marks at the lower edge and center. This will ensure that both curves are identical. Construct and attach the cuff like a standard barrel cuff, then fold in half and press.

Collars

While you can always just hem or face the neck edge opening of a garment, a collar can add both a decorative and functional finish.

Basic Collar

A basic or standard collar consists of two pieces, an upper collar and an under collar. The under collar is what gets attached to the neck edge of a shirt and has a small button and buttonhole. The upper collar is attached to the under collar and is folded down toward the shirt. Points on the upper collar can be altered to make them either closer together or further apart, but they are still constructed the same.

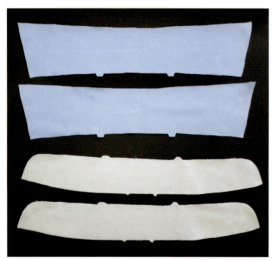

1. Start by cutting out two upper and two under collar pattern pieces, transferring all notches and marks.

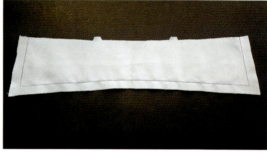

2. Along the sides and un-notched edge of the upper collar, stitch using a ⅝" (1.6cm) seam allowance.

3. Clip the corners, and then turn right side out and press.

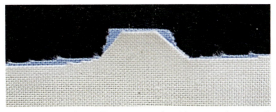 

4. With the under-collar pieces right sides together, sandwich the upper collar between them. Align the raw edges and notches, and ensure that the ends of the upper collar are aligned with the marks on the under collar. Pin in place, then stitch using a ⅝" (1.6cm) seam allowance, starting and stopping the stitching ⅝" (1.6cm) from the lower edge.

5. Trim the seam allowance along the curves by half, then turn the under collar right side out and press.

6. To attach the collar to the neck opening, align the notches and pin one side of the under collar with the right side of the garment fabric.

7. Along the edge of the under collar that was left unstitched in step 4, fold the fabric ⅝" (1.6cm) toward the wrong side. This will make the folded ends of the under collar align with the edges of the neck opening. Stitch in place using a ⅝" (1.6cm) seam allowance.

8. Along the remaining raw edge of the under collar, fold and press ⅝" (1.6cm) toward the wrong side. With the seam allowance of the under collar and garment neck edge folded toward the under collar, position the folded edge of the under collar over the previous line of stitching and pin in place.

9. Topstitch in place ⅛" (3.2mm) from the edge or hand stitch in place using an invisible stitch.

Mandarin Collar

A mandarin collar is a stand-up style of collar and essentially looks like you've only attached the under collar of a standard collar to the neck edge of the garment.

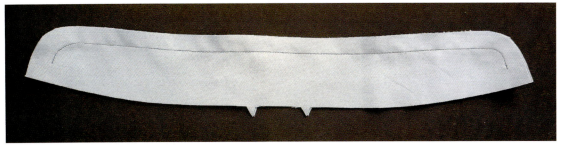

1. Start by cutting out two collar pieces. Align the pieces with right sides together and stitch the upper edge and sides using a ⅝" (1.6cm) seam allowance, starting and ending the stitching ⅝" (1.6cm) from the lower edge.

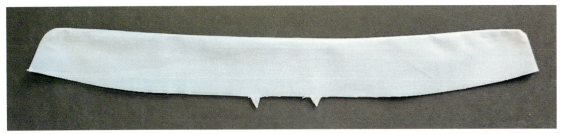

2. Trim the seam allowance along the curves by half, then turn the collar right side out and press. Attach the collar to the neck opening of a garment, just like the under collar of a basic collar.

Tip!

When cutting out pieces from fabric that can't be pinned, use fabric weights to hold the pattern pieces in place.

Techniques / Collars

Peter Pan Collar

A Peter Pan collar is a collar that is wider than a standard collar and has a founded edge.

1. Start by cutting out two collar pieces. Align the pieces with right sides together and stitch the longer curved edge using a ⅝" (1.6cm) seam allowance, starting and ending the stitching ⅝" (1.6cm) from the upper edge.

2. Trim the seam allowance along the curves by half, then turn the collar right side out and press.

3. Attach the collar to the neck opening of a garment just like the under collar of a basic collar.

Trick!

Guarantee two identically shaped collar pieces every time! First, cut one shaped collar from fabric and apply fusible interfacing to the wrong side, ensuring that the interfacing is aligned with the stitching lines of the collar. Mark the grainline on the interfacing for reference. With right sides together, and following the grainline arrow, align the cut collar with a second piece of fabric. Stitch the lower curved edge of the collar along the interfacing edge, then cut the second collar layer from fabric. Clip the curves, then turn right side out and press. The collar is ready to be used!

Peter Pan-style collars can also be made as stand-alone pieces and worn like necklaces.

1. To do this, cut the pattern piece in half at the center back, then add seam allowances and cut the pieces from fabric.

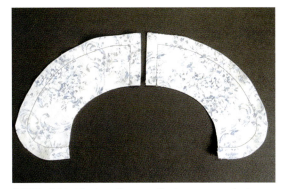

2. With right sides together, sew the longer curved edges and center back using a ⅝" (1.6cm) seam allowance.

3. Trim the seam allowance along the curves by half, then turn right-side out and press. Along the raw edges, fold the fabric ¼" (6.4mm) toward the wrong side and press. Align the folded edges and topstitch in place ⅛" (3.2mm) from the edge.

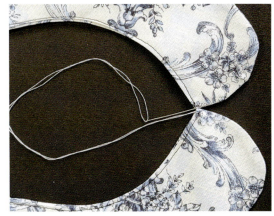

4. Secure the center front with a small hand stitch. At the center back, sew a hook and eye or other preferred closure. (See page 142 for hook and eye.)

Elastic

Whether it's inserted into the waistband of a pair of pants, used as the waistband of a skirt, or added to the lower edge of a sleeve, there's an elastic type for every application.

Braided Elastic

Braided elastic is elastic made of multiple strands of rubber or latex threads that are braided together. This gives it the look of several lines of parallel ribs down its length. Braided elastic is fairly strong and durable and comes in a variety of widths. However, it can lose its strength when pierced with a needle. This makes it a better choice for inserting into a waistband or similar casing as opposed to sewing along an edge.

Woven Elastic

Woven elastic is made by weaving synthetic fibers like polyester, spandex, or nylon together. It comes in a variety of widths, and it is considered one of the strongest types of elastic. It is also commonly referred to as no-roll elastic, meaning that the edges won't fold over or roll when stretched.

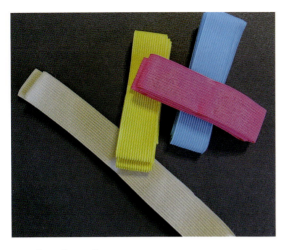

Knit Elastic

Knit elastic is made from synthetic fibers of either polyester or rubber knit together. Knit elastic is very soft and comfortable against the skin, making it a great elastic choice for undergarments.

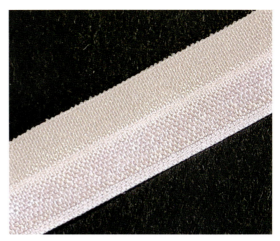

Fold-Over Elastic

Fold-over elastic, as the name implies, can easily be folded over the edge of a project along its center crease. It can be made from a variety of different materials and comes in a variety of widths.

Swim Elastic

Swim elastic is elastic meant specifically for swimwear. It is made from either rubber or a combination of cotton and rubber and is chemically treated to withstand chlorine and salt water. Swim elastic can either be different colors or clear.

Buttonhole Elastic

Buttonhole elastic is elastic made with a series of holes down the center. It is commonly used along waistbands in children's clothing to allow for adjustable sizes.

Quarter Marking

Quarter marking is the process of marking four equal quadrants in a circumference of elastic. The same marks are made on the circumference of the garment that the elastic is being sewn to, like a waistband. The marks on the elastic are then aligned and pinned with the marks of the garments. As the elastic is stitched to the garment, it is stretched between the pins until it lays flat along the fabric. This results in evenly distributed fabric along the elastic.

Inserting Elastic

If elastic is being inserted into a garment or project, it is generally done so in a casing.

1. A simple casing can made by folding and pressing the upper edge of a fabric by ¼" (6.4mm), and then folding the edge over again approximately ¼" (6.4mm) wider than the elastic that will be inserted into the casing and sewing in place close to the lower fold.

2. Insert the elastic into the casing by attaching either a safety pin or a bodkin to one end and feeding it through.

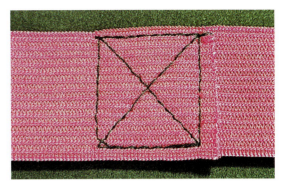

Join Elastic Ends: Zigzag Stitch

Depending on where the elastic is being used in a project, you may need to join the ends, like when sewing a waistband. A simple way to join the ends is to simply overlap the ends by approximately ½" (1.2cm), then run a zigzag stitch back and forth down the center of the overlapped ends.

Join Elastic Ends: Square Stitch

If you know the elastic that is being joined is going to undergo a lot of repeated stress, a sturdier way to attach the ends is to overlap the ends by approximately 1" (2.5cm) and sew a square around the overlapped edges. Then, sew an X through the center of the square for added strength.

Join Elastic Ends: No-Bulk Stitch

If you don't want the added bulk of overlapping the elastic ends, they can be joined using fabric instead.

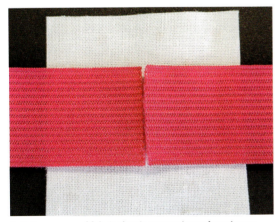

1. Cut a square of fabric that is approximately twice as wide as the elastic. Center the elastic ends on the fabric square with the ends next to one another.

2. Wrap the fabric around the elastic, then sew in place along the fabric ends and the center where the elastic edges are aligned using a zigzag stitch.

Stabilizer and Interfacing

Stabilizer and interfacing are both used in a variety of different applications, from garment construction to embroidery, and while they are similar, they cannot always be used interchangeably. Stabilizer is used when embroidering or sewing a seam on stretchy fabric and the excess around the stitching is meant to be removed once the stitching is done. Interfacing is used to add stiffness to a fabric and is meant to be a permanent addition to the fabric.

Cut-Away Stabilizer

Cut-away stabilizer is a stabilizer that can be cut away from a project after stitching is complete. It can come in a variety of weights, from light to heavy, and the weight you choose to use can depend on the fabric being stitched and the project. Cut-away stabilizers are good to use if the fabric you are embroidering or stitching on has stretch and you want to keep the embroidered area stabilized, even after wearing and laundering.

Tear-Away Stabilizer

Tear-away stabilizer is stabilizer that can be easily torn away from the edges of stitching once it is complete. It is generally only meant to give stability to a fabric during the stitching process, not to maintain the stability afterwards like cut-away stabilizer will.

Tip!

Use tissue paper or a tear-away stabilizer on the top and bottom of knit or other stretch fabrics to keep them from stretching as you sew. A walking foot or roller foot can also help prevent the fabric from stretching.

Wash-Away Stabilizer

Wash-away stabilizer is a water-soluble stabilizer that will dissolve and wash away after stitching is done. This type of stabilizer is ideal for lighter-weight fabrics or for embroidering lace.

Woven Interfacing

Woven interfacing is made by weaving thin fibers together, similar to a woven fabric. It comes in a variety of weights and is meant to add both thickness and strength to a fabric. Because woven interfacing has grain, just like woven fabric, you will want the grain to be the same direction as the fabric.

Non-Woven Interfacing

Non-woven interfacing is made from bonded fibers and has no grain. Because of this, it is less durable than woven interfacing. Non-woven interfacing comes in a variety of weights, doesn't ravel when cut, and doesn't shrink when laundered.

Knit Interfacing

Knit interfacing is made by knitting fibers together, which means it has some stretch to it. It can be added to knit fabric to provide extra strength and thickness while still allowing the fabric to stretch.

Sew-in and Fusible

All types of interfacing come in either sew-in or fusible varieties. Sew-in interfacing acts like a second layer of fabric and is attached to a project at the seams. It is generally used on fabrics that cannot be pressed or on garments where you want the fabric to maintain its natural drape. Fusible interfacing has a fusible adhesive on one side that sticks to the wrong side of fabric when pressed. It is a great option when you want stiffness through an entire area of a project or garment, like the bottom of a bag or the collars and cuffs of a garment.

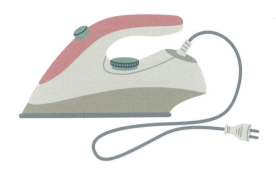

Pressing vs. Ironing

An important distinction to know when adding fusible interfacing to a fabric is the difference between pressing and ironing. Pressing is the act of placing an iron down on a surface, leaving it for a few seconds, and then taking it completely off the fabric before moving it to another area and setting it down again. Ironing is the process of moving the iron back and forth along a garment or piece of fabric. While ironing is fine to do on your clothes to get rid of wrinkles, when adding a fusible interfacing to a fabric, it can distort both the fabric and the interfacing.

Tip!

Interfacing comes in different colors too! Generally, it comes in both a light and a dark variety, so pick the one that best matches your fabric.

Trick!

Turning a project right side out and being able to press out a perfect point without pushing through the fabric can be tricky. One way to overcome this is to pull your corners out, rather than push them.

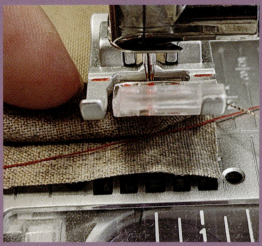

1. Sew the seam along one fabric edge with your normal stitch length. As you approach the corner, reduce the stitch length slightly, then stop one stitch from the corner with the needle down. Place a length of thread between the layers of fabric and pull the thread slightly so that it is right up against the needle. You want the next stitch to go over the thread, not through it.

2. Take one stitch, then pull the right-hand side of the thread to the left.

3. Keeping the thread sandwiched between the fabric layers, pivot the fabric to begin stitching down the next side. Take one to two stitches and lengthen the stitch length back to your normal length and stitch the remainder of the seam. Trim the seam allowances and clip the corner, then turn the fabric right side out and gently tug on the thread ends to pull the corner into a perfect point.

4. Holding onto one end of the thread, pull it out from between the seams.

Fusible Web

Fusible web is a double-sided fusible adhesive, not to be confused with interfacing or stabilizer. It is used to hold two layers of fabric together. It has a paper backing on one side and small adhesive dots on the other.

1. Draw or trace a shape on the paper side of the fusible web and roughly cut out. Place the fusible web adhesive-side down on the wrong side of a fabric and press, following the manufacturer's instructions for iron heat settings and pressing time.

2. Cut out the shape, then remove the paper backing to reveal the adhesive now on the fabric.

3. Place the fabric adhesive-side down on another fabric and press in place. The layers will now be permanently adhered together.

Stay Tape

Stay tape is a pre-cut strip of fusible interfacing. It comes in a variety of weights and widths and can be added along the seamline of a fabric prior to sewing to keep it from stretching or distorting.

Tip!

Don't confuse stay tape with hem tape! Stay tape has adhesive on only one side of the strip, while hem tape has adhesive on both.

Techniques / Stabilizer and Interfacing

Seams

Seams come in all different widths, lengths, and shapes, and while straight seams are easier, others have their place in projects too.

Curved Seam

A curved seam can seem tricky at first, but if you take it slow, you can maintain an even seam allowance around the curved edge of a fabric. When sewing curved seams, if possible, set your machine to automatically stop with the needle down when you let off the presser foot. This will allow you to make small pivots and corrections to the fabric to get you around the curve without moving off the desired seam allowance. Drawing the seam allowance onto the fabric can also make it easier to sew, as opposed to trying to follow a seam allowance mark on the throat plate of a machine.

If the fabric pieces you are sewing do not have the same amount of curve to them, always sew with the smaller piece or the piece with the most amount of curve on the top. This will allow you to see if there are any puckers in the fabric that might get sewn into the seam and adjust before they do.

Hack!
Everything from seam allowance stickers to rubber bands, and even magnets and mounting tape can be used to mark seam allowances on a sewing machine.

Tip!

When sewing curved seams, only worry about the fabric directly under the needle. The fabric to the left of the presser foot may have wrinkles and puckers, but don't let them distract you. As long as the fabric under the needle is lying flat, you won't have any puckers or gathers in the stitched seam.

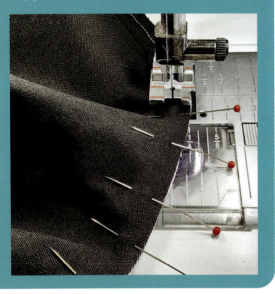

Partial Seam

A partial seam is a technique where you sew part of a seam together first, then sew another section of fabric together before going back and finishing the first seam.

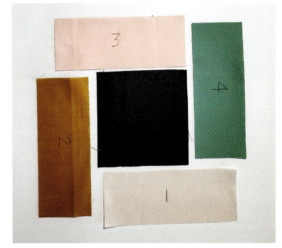

1. First, identify where a partial seam is needed by laying out the fabric pieces to be stitched. In this example, a partial seam will be needed along the inner edge of the first rectangle to stitch the square into the center.

Tip!

When cutting notches along a long, curved edge, consider using pinking shears to get the job done quicker and easier!

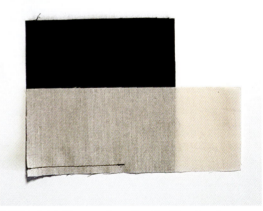

2. With right sides together, align the #1 rectangle approximately with the center square. Using a ¼" (6.4mm) seam allowance, stitch from the fabric edge to the center of the rectangle, backstitching at the beginning and end.

Techniques / Seams

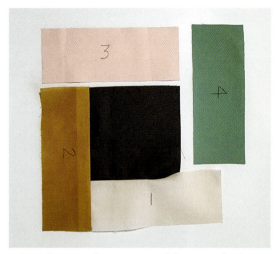 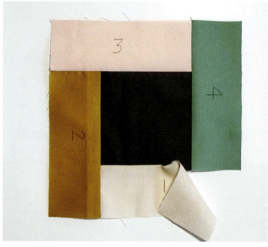

3. Press the seam allowance toward the rectangle, then align the #2 rectangle with the next edge of the square and rectangle, with right sides together, and stitch in place using a ¼" (6.4mm) seam allowance.

4. Sew the #3 rectangle in place using a ¼" (6.4mm) seam allowance, press the seam allowance toward the rectangle, then repeat to sew the #4 rectangle in place as well.

 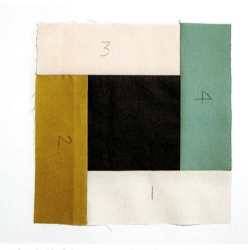

5. With the #4 rectangle in place, realign the #1 rectangle with the other half of the square and the lower edge of the #4 rectangle, and finish sewing the remainder of the first seam.

Tip!

Always set your seam before pressing it open or to one side. Do this by pressing the seam how the fabric came off the machine—for example, with right sides together. This sets the thread into the fabric so that when the fabric is opened and the seam allowance is pressed, it will lay nice and flat.

Nesting Seam

Nesting seams is a way to perfectly align two seams on top of one another and reduce the bulk of the resulting seam. To nest a seam, simply press the seam allowances of the seams to be aligned in opposite directions. When you align the seam, the opposing seam allowances will nest together against one another.

Tip!

When nesting seams, always place the pin in the second seam allowance, or the one that is closest to you when the seam being sewn is on the machine. This will allow you to stitch over the seam you want aligned before you have to remove the pin.

Openwork Seam

An openwork seam is a technique for joining the edges of fabric together with a space in between. The fabric edges will be folded and pressed toward the wrong side, if the fabric ravels, and they will generally be stitched with a zigzag or decorative stitch.

Stiffened Seam

A stiffened seam is a seam that has been reinforced so that it maintains its shape. This can be done with fusible interfacing or stay tape, or with a product called boning. Boning is a narrow, rigid strip of plastic or metal that is inserted into a seam to add structure. It is commonly found on garments like dresses or corsets.

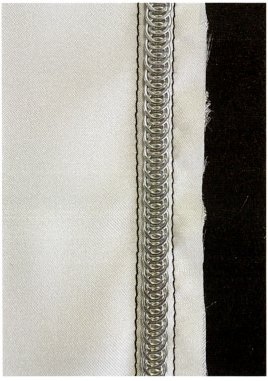

1. Start by sewing a standard ⅝" seam allowance. Next, sew a parallel line of stitching along the seam allowance that is roughly 1/16" (1.6mm) wider than the boning width to create a narrow casing.

2. Insert the boning into the casing. The seam can then be folded to one side.

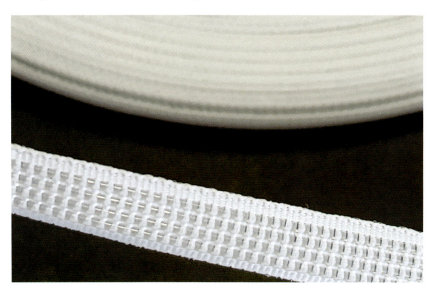

3. Boning also comes in a slightly less-stiff option. It comes with two narrow strips of fabric along either side of a hardened piece of plastic. You can simply sew this boning into a seam allowance along the fabric edge.

Other Ways to Embellish Fabric

While fabric can be found with any number of different embellishments already on the surface, from beads to sequins to decorative trim, there are several other ways to add both visual interest and texture to a fabric.

Appliqué

Appliqué is the technique of placing one fabric on top of another and stitching around the edge of the top fabric to secure. Generally, the top fabric will be cut in a specific shape or design and the perimeter of it can be stitched using a variety of different stitches, from zigzag to blanket to decorative.

Hack!

Clothespins can be used to cleanly store lengths of binding, piping, ribbon, and other embellishments.

Reverse Appliqué

Reverse appliqué is the technique of cutting away a fabric to reveal another one underneath.

> ## Tip!
> When using an appliqué stitch like a blanket stitch, always stop with the needle down in the background fabric when adjusting the fabric. This will keep the stitches going into the appliqué shape on top of one another as opposed to making a small V shape.

1. Layer two pieces of fabric together, both with the right sides up. Stitch any desired, close-ended shape into the layers of fabric using a shortened stitching length like 1.5mm.

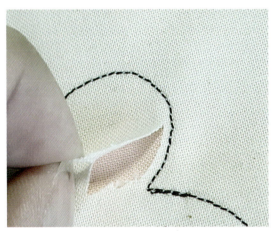

2. Just inside the stitching line, cut away the top layer of fabric to reveal the fabric underneath.

Hack!
Some embellishments come on netting. Rather than using a pair of scissors to cut the netting away, which can leave small threads behind, use a hot knife. Cutting around the embellishment edge with the hot knife will not only sever the threads, but it will seal the ends as well.

Techniques / Other Ways to Embellish Fabric

Shadow Appliqué

Shadow appliqué is the technique of layering a sheer fabric like organza over an appliqué to create a muted look.

1. Cut out and adhere your appliqué shapes to a background fabric using fusible web or another adhesive.

2. Layer a piece of sheer fabric over the appliqué shapes and background fabric and stitch the perimeter of the shapes using your desired stitch.

Trick!

Whether it's a tie on the front of a jacket or the waistband of a skirt, tie the bow so that it's always straight with the tail ends hanging down.

1. With the tie wrapped around you, start by taking the right side (which will now be referred to as Side A) over the left side (which will now be referred to as Side B), then under it to tie a knot.

2. Fold Side A under on itself to create a small loop and hold the loop to the right.

3. Fold Side B over on itself to create a small loop.

4. Pass the loop of Side B under the top layer of Side A.

5. Pull the loops to tighten the bow and straighten if needed.

Techniques / Other Ways to Embellish Fabric

Couching

Couching is the process of sewing over thick thread, yarn, cord, or other trim to secure it to the surface of a fabric. This can be done using a zigzag or other decorative stitch in either matching or contrasting thread colors.

Bobbin Work

Bobbin work is the technique of using heavier threads or yarn in the bobbin as you sew. This allows you to sew with things that won't fit through the eye of a needle! Bobbin work will either create beautiful stitches on the wrong side of a project so that it can be reversible, or you can sew with the wrong side of a project up so that the stitching is on the right side when it is completed. Depending on your machine, this technique may require you to loosen the bobbin tension on your machine. Consult your machine manual on how to do this. If you plan to use this technique often and aren't comfortable loosening and tightening your bobbin tension repeatedly, consider getting an extra bobbin case for your machine that is only for bobbin work!

1. Wind the thread or yarn onto the bobbin by hand.

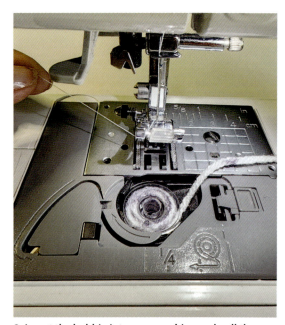

2. Insert the bobbin into your machine and pull the thread or yarn from the bobbin through the needle plate of the machine to start. To do this, pull a length of thread through the needle and hold it to the left.

 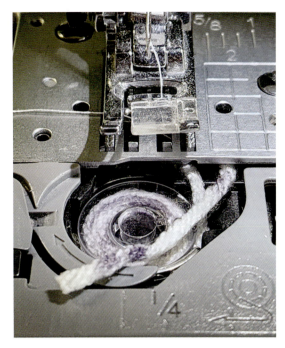

 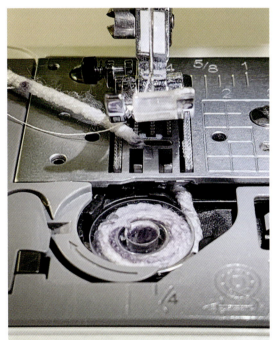

3. Turn the handwheel of the machine toward you one full rotation. This will take the needle thread around the bobbin, catch the yarn in the bobbin, and allow you to pull it up through the throat plate opening.

Techniques / Other Ways to Embellish Fabric

4. Using a straight stitch with a slightly longer stitch length, like a 2.8mm or 3.0mm, run a short line of test stitches. If the fabric is bunching as you sew, loosen the bobbin tension slightly and then sew again. Continue stitching and adjusting until the fabric lays flat as you sew.

5. Once the tension of the stitching is correct, simply sew! You can sew in simple straight lines, curvy lines, or outline a design.

Tip!

This technique works best on medium-to-heavier-weight woven fabric. If using a lighter-weight fabric, stabilize the wrong side of the fabric using your preferred stabilizer.

Hack!

A small hair elastic can be used to keep bobbins from unwinding.

Tip!

Not every machine uses the same bobbin type and size. If you are buying more bobbins for your machine, or considering buying pre-wound bobbins, be sure to consult your machine manual to see what kind to get. Trying to use the wrong size or type of bobbin in your machine can cause stitch-quality issues and may even harm the machine.

Hack!

Keep your matching bobbins and thread together using an elastic! Loop the elastic through the center of the bobbin, then wrap it around the spool of thread to keep them together.

Hack!

A toe separator, normally used during a pedicure, can also be used to keep bobbins from unwinding!

Techniques / Other Ways to Embellish Fabric

Trapunto

Trapunto, also known as stuffed work, is the technique of creating a raised, puffy design on the surface of fabric with batting or stuffing.

1. One way to do this is to layer two pieces of fabric together. The top fabric will be seen and should be right-side up, while the second fabric will be hidden on the wrong side. Stitch the perimeter of a shape or a close-ended design.

2. In the fabric on the wrong side, make small slits in the center of the shape of the design through that fabric only—do not cut through the fabric on the right side.

3. Using small amounts of fiberfill stuffing at a time, stuff the shape or design, then secure the slit opening with several hand stitches.

4. Once the designs have all been stuffed, layer the fabric with a lining or other piece of fabric. The fabric can be held together at the seam of whatever project is being constructed, or additional lines of stitching can be made through the layers of fabric outside the trapunto design to make the puffy area even more prominent.

Hack!

If you have several spools of ribbon or other embellishments to store, place several dowels through the holes in a basket and slide them on. Everything is organized, easy to see, and can be spooled off their rolls without having to take them off the dowels.

Techniques / Other Ways to Embellish Fabric

Patterns

If you've been sewing for any length of time, you've probably made (or wanted to make) some kind of garment. Whatever the reason, knowing how to read patterns is a great skill to have.

Pattern Markings 118

Lines 121

Measurements 124

Pattern Markings

Whether you are buying a commercial pattern from a big box store or downloading one from an independent designer online, there are several commonly used markings you should know.

Notches

Notches on patterns are small triangles that help you accurately align pieces. For example, you will commonly find notches on front and side front pieces for shirts. These notches should be aligned when sewing this seam.

When cutting out pattern pieces from fabric, at the notch, you simply cut the

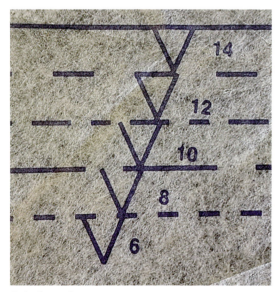

A single notch.

A double notch.

118   500 Sewing Tips, Tricks, Techniques, and Hacks

On this sleeve pattern, you can see the differences between the single and double notches.

small triangle into the seam allowance. If you find that this is too hard to see, you can also cut the triangle away from the seam allowance and trim it off after the seam is complete.

Single notches are used on the front of a pattern, while double notches are used on the back. For example, double notches are used to align two back pieces for a center back seam.

It is important to note the difference between single and double notches, especially on sleeve pattern pieces, so that you don't accidentally sew a sleeve in backwards.

Circles

There are two main types of circle markings on patterns: open circles, and circles with a cross through the middle. The open circles are used to show you where pattern pieces should align with one another. For example, circles on a shirt-front pattern piece should align with the upper corners of a pocket pattern piece.

The waistline pattern piece is marked with a circle with a cross through the middle.

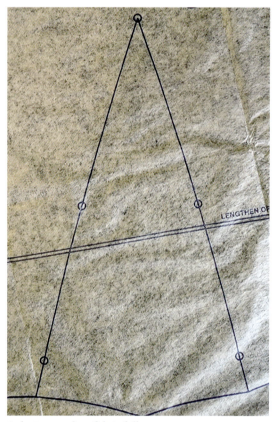

A dart can reduce fabric fullness.

Circles with a cross through the middle are used to show where a pattern piece is designed to fall on a certain area of the body. For example, a waistline, bust apex (the fullest part of the bust), or the hip.

Circle markings can be transferred from a pattern to fabric by using either a removable fabric marker or by using a tailor's tack.

Circles can also be used to show where a dart should start and stop. When folding a dart, the circles across from one another should align.

Hack!

Freezer paper can be used as a reusable template for marking or cutting fabric. Simply draw your pattern shape onto the dull side of the paper and cut it out. Place the freezer paper waxy-side down on the fabric and iron in place with a dry iron set to low heat. The freezer paper will stick to the fabric so that you can cut out the shape, and it can then be easily and cleanly peeled away. The freezer paper template will last for multiple uses.

Lines

Several types of lines can be used throughout a pattern, and while most of them are universal, it's always a good idea to look at the pattern instructions to ensure what the lines are for.

Size Lines

Most patterns come with a range of different sizes all printed together. The different sizes are noted by dashed lines of different lengths. Once you select the size of pattern you want to use, follow that dashed line when cutting out the pieces.

Grainline

A long line with a triangle or arrow at one end shows the grainline direction of a pattern piece. When placing the pattern piece on fabric, the line should be parallel to the grainline of the fabric.

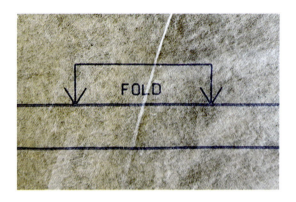

Cut on Fold Line

A long line with two arrows perpendicular to the ends of the line indicate where a pattern piece needs to be cut on a fold. Prior to pinning the pattern piece to the fabric, fold the fabric in half, then align the "cut on fold" line with the folded edge of the fabric.

Tip!

When cutting out larger pattern pieces, for example a jacket front or a pant leg, ensure that the entire pattern piece is on the cutting surface, not hanging off the edge. If the fabric is hanging off the edge of the cutting surface, the pattern piece shape could unintentionally become distorted.

Lengthen and Shorten Lines

Two parallel lines very close to one another indicate where a pattern can be lengthened or shortened. These lines are commonly found on the front and back of shirt pattern pieces as well as sleeves. It is important to only lengthen or shorten in these areas, as it will ensure that no other design element of a pattern piece is affected—for example, the curve at the bottom hem of a shirt or the placket on a sleeve.

Additional Lines and Markings

There should essentially be a mark on a pattern piece for every aspect of a garment. For example, if there is a pleat, there should be a line with an arrow telling you what direction to fold it. If there are buttons and buttonholes required on a garment, there should be lines or Xs telling you where they go. While all these pattern markings should tell you everything you need to know about cutting, prepping, aligning, and assembling a garment, always read the pattern assembly instructions if you don't know what a marking is for—don't just ignore it!

Lines and other markings on patterns will guide you in making the perfect garment.

Hack!
Heavy, oversized washers make great pattern weights!

Tip!
Use a low-heat iron with no steam to flatten commercial pattern pieces straight from the package. This not only makes them easier to cut out, but cutting fabric pieces following a flat pattern with no folds or wrinkles is more accurate.

Tip!
If you have a commercial pattern that you really like and plan on using over and over, consider fusing lightweight interfacing to the wrong side of the pattern to make it stiffer and allow it to hold up to repetitive use.

Measurements

Before you can start cutting out pattern pieces and assembling a garment, you have to know what size to make. To do that, you need to take accurate body measurements. The first step to doing this is using a flexible fiberglass measuring tape. This tape will easily curve around your body but won't stretch—giving the most accurate measurements possible.

When taking your own body measurements, it can be helpful to stand in front of a full-length mirror. This way, you can see if the measuring tape in is the correct position and see whether it is perfectly perpendicular or parallel to your body in the areas being measured. Be sure not to pull the measuring tape tight around your body when measuring; rather, the tape should be just snug. Don't wear bulky clothes when taking measurements and don't try to "suck" in your waist. Having the most accurate measurement to begin with will help ensure that the final garment fits.

Where to Measure

Most commercial sewing patterns have three main areas of measurement that can be used to determine pattern size; bust, waist, and hip. The bust measurement should be taken under the arms, across the back, and around the fullest part of the bust. The waist measurement should be taken around the body at the natural waist, or the narrowest part of the waist. The hip measurement should be taken around the body at the fullest part of the hips.

Another common measurement used when selecting a pattern size is a back length measurement, or a back neck to waist measurement. This measurement is taken from the base of the neck to the natural waist. When making pants, another measurement you will need to take is the inseam measurement. This measurement is made from the crotch to the ankle bone.

Grading Between Pattern Sizes

Once you have all these measurements and you select a pattern to use, you may find that they don't all align in one size. For example, you could be a size 8 in the bust, a size 10 in the waist, and a size 12 in the hips. While there are many different types of alterations that can be made to certain areas of a pattern to make them larger or smaller, a quick and easy way to get the pattern closer to the correct size in all areas is to grade between the size lines.

Do this by using a long, straight ruler or curved ruler, and drawing a new pattern line to follow when cutting that starts at the size 8 line in the bust and ends at the size 10 line in the waist. Then, continue drawing the new line starting at the size 10 line in the waist and ending at the size 12 line in the hips.

Lengthening and Shortening

One of the easiest alterations to do on a pattern is to make it longer or shorter. There will be lines on a pattern piece that show you where this can be done. It is important to make this alteration only in these areas so that no other design element of the garment is changed.

To make a garment shorter, simply cut along the lengthen/shorten line and overlap the pattern pieces. Depending on how much you are overlapping the cut edges, you will need to true up the sides of the pattern pieces. Do this by using either a straight-edge or a French-curve ruler, depending on the pattern piece, and redrawing new, straight lines.

To make a garment longer, simply cut along the lengthen/shorten line and spread the pattern pieces apart. Place a new piece of pattern paper under the cut edges and tape in place. Using the correct ruler, draw new lines to connect the pattern pieces, then cut off the excess pattern paper.

Trick!

Remove the bed of your sewing machine when hemming pants or sewing other small tubes. This allows you to slide the fabric tube over the machine and keep it lying flat under the needle as you sew.

Closures

Whether you are making garments, accessories, or home décor projects, you are bound to need a fastener at some point to hold parts and pieces of fabric together. From zippers to snaps, grommets to frogs, there's a fastener for every project and application.

Zippers............................... 128

Fasteners 139

Buttons 144

Zippers

A zipper is one of the most versatile closures and can be added to everything from bags to jackets to pillows. Zippers come in a variety of lengths, colors, and teeth material like nylon, metal, or molded plastic. The type of zipper tooth material you choose to use will depend on the project you are sewing. A more robust project requires a stronger zipper.

All-Purpose Zipper

An all-purpose zipper can be used on anything from garments to home décor projects or accessories. They are generally a nylon tape and have coil teeth. They are lightweight, flexible, and come in a variety of lengths.

Metal Zipper

Metal zippers are zippers with metal teeth. They are very strong and commonly used in garments made from heavier fabrics like denim.

Molded Plastic Zipper

Molded plastic zippers have larger teeth made of molded plastic. They are heavier duty than coil zippers and are commonly used on garments like jackets or accessories like bags.

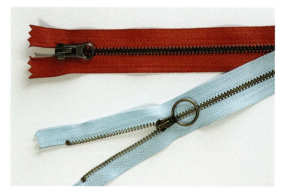

Invisible Zipper

Invisible zippers have coil teeth that are not visible from the right side of the zipper. When correctly sewn into a project, they are invisible, making them a great choice for garments such as skirts and dresses.

Two-Way Zipper

A two-way zipper is a zipper that has a pull on either end, meaning it can be opened or closed from either end. Two-way zippers can be made with either coils, molded plastic, or metal teeth and are commonly used on larger projects like duffle bags.

Separating Zipper

A separating zipper is one that allows both sides of the zipper tape to come apart and then easily be rejoined. They can be made with either coils, molded plastic, or metal teeth and are commonly used in jackets, coats, and vests.

Decorative Tape Zipper

As the name suggests, this type of zipper has a decorative tape. They can be made with either coils, molded plastic, or metal teeth and come in a variety of colors, prints, and materials. These zippers are generally added to the right side of a project so that the entire tape is visible.

Closures / Zippers

Decorative Tooth Zipper

Zippers can also be made with decorative teeth! This can be anything from different colors of metal to rhinestones added to molded plastic teeth.

Sewing Zippers

There are several different ways to insert zippers depending on the project and the zipper. To simply sew a zipper to fabric, start by installing a zipper foot onto the machine.

1. With right sides together, and the zipper partially open, align the fabric and zipper tape and pin in place.

2. With the wrong side of the zipper tape up, and the zipper foot against the edge of the zipper teeth, sew along one side of the zipper, starting at the upper edge of the zipper and stopping when you get close to the opened zipper pull.

3. With the needle down, raise the presser foot and zip the zipper closed. This will move the zipper pull past the needle.

4. Continue stitching the rest of the way down the zipper.

5. Depending on your zipper foot, either move the zipper foot to the other attachment point or adjust your needle position to sew on the other side of the zipper. Repeat steps 1–4 to sew another piece of fabric to the remaining side of the zipper tape. Topstitch if desired.

Standard Zipper with Basted Fabric

Depending on the project you are making and the zipper you are using, you may want the zipper tape and teeth to be more hidden by fabric. A quick and easy way to do this is to baste the fabric together first. This method will attach the zipper and topstitch the fabric at the same time.

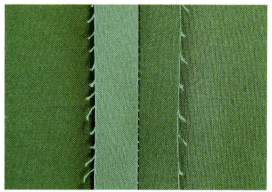

1. Sew the seam up to where the zipper will be inserted with a regular stitch length, backstitch, then cut the threads. Lengthen the stitch length to 4mm and baste the seam where the zipper will be inserted. Do not backstitch at the beginning or end. Press the seam allowances open.

2. Place the right side of the zipper tape against the pressed seam allowances on the wrong side of the fabric with the zipper tape centered over the basted seam. Pin in place.

3. Using a zipper foot and the same method as before (step 3 on page 131) for stitching around the zipper pull, stitch down one side of the zipper, across the bottom of the zipper tape below the teeth, and then back up the other side of the zipper.

4. Remove the basting stitches.

Invisible Zipper

A popular zipper to use in garments like skirts or blouses is an invisible zipper, because, as the name suggests, it cannot be seen while the garment is worn.

1. To sew an invisible zipper, first start by pressing the zipper tape. Open the zipper and, with an iron set on medium heat, press the zipper tape up to the coil so that it lays flat. Do not press directly on top of the zipper coil as it could melt; you are just trying to take the slight curl out of the zipper tape. This will allow you to stitch closer to the zipper coil and keep the zipper as invisible as possible.

2. With right sides together and the zipper open, pin the zipper tape to the fabric. The coil of the zipper should be right along the seam allowance being used in the project. For most garments, this is ⅝" (1.6cm). If it's easier, you can mark the seam allowance with a removable fabric marker prior to placing the zipper.

3. Starting at the top of the zipper, stitch as close to the zipper coil as possible using a zipper foot, stopping just before the zipper pull. Because you are sewing so close to the narrow coil of the zipper, it can be nearly impossible to try and zip the zipper past the presser foot while the project is on the machine.

4. Repeat steps 2 and 3 to pin and stitch the other side of the zipper tape to another piece of fabric, again ensuring that the zipper coil is aligned along the seam allowance, and stitching as close to the zipper coil as possible.

5. Close the zipper and then sew the remainder of the unstitched zipper as close to the coils as possible. If you struggle to do this by machine, this small length of stitches can be done by hand using a backstitch.

Lapped Zipper

A lapped zipper is another way to sew a zipper into a project so that the tape and teeth are hidden.

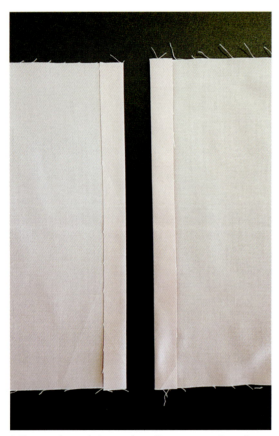

1. To sew a lapped zipper, along the seam opening where the zipper will be inserted, press the seam allowance width of fabric toward the wrong side. Lapped zippers are commonly used in garments, so a ⅝" (1.6cm) seam allowance would be used.

2. With the fabric and zipper tape right side up and the zipper halfway open, align the left side of the zipper tape on the wrong side of the fabric so that the zipper teeth are right along the edge of the pressed seam allowance. Pin in place.

3. Using a zipper foot, stitch along the edge of the zipper approximately ⅛" (3.2mm) away from the pressed edge of the fabric.

4. When you reach the zipper pull, stop with the needle down in the fabric, raise the presser foot, and zip the zipper closed. Continue stitching the remainder of the zipper.

5. With the zipper closed, align the pressed edge of the next piece of fabric with the previous stitching line. This fabric will cover the zipper teeth.

6. Stitch approximately ½" (1.2cm) from the pressed edge of the fabric. This side of the seam allowance will become the lapped edge that covers the zipper tape.

Closures / Zippers

Zipper Tab

Depending on your project, there may come a time where the zipper opening does not match up with an available length of zipper, and you must shorten the zipper. An easy way to do this is to create a zipper tab on the stopper end of the zipper. This can also be done as a decorative addition to a zipper.

2. Along the sides of the zipper tab, fold and press the fabric toward the wrong side until the raw edges align in the center.

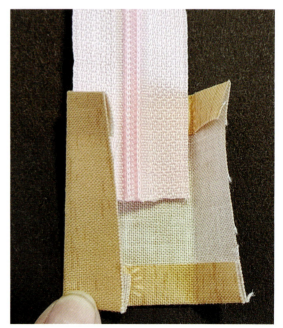

1. Cut a rectangle of fabric that is twice the width of the zipper tape and 2 ½ times longer than you want the zipper tab to be. Along the upper and lower edge of the fabric rectangle, fold and press the fabric ¼" (6.4mm) toward the wrong side.

3. With the wrong side of the zipper up, insert the cut end of the zipper tape into the pressed rectangle until the edge of the tape is at the center of the rectangle.

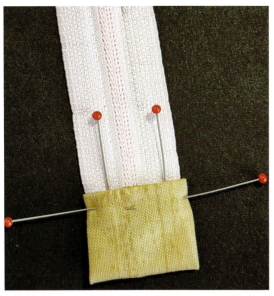

4. Fold the rectangle in half over the zipper tape, aligning the upper and lower edges as well as the pressed sides. Pin in place.

5. Stitch the perimeter of the zipper tab approximately 1/8" (3.2mm) from the edge. When stitching over the zipper teeth, use the hand wheel of the machine to slowly advance the needle. This will help eliminate the chance of bending or breaking a needle.

Window Zipper Opening

A window zipper opening is an easy way to attach fabric to a zipper when you need a zipper opening in what will be the top layer of stitched fabric, like in a bag or pouch.

Closures / Zippers

1. To make a window zipper opening, draw the desired rectangle opening on the wrong side of the fabric, ensuring that the opening is not wider or longer than the zipper tape.

  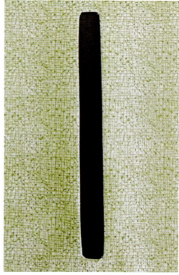

2. Starting and ending approximately ¼" (6.4mm) from the ends of the rectangle, draw a line down the center of the rectangle. At the ends of the center line, draw diagonal lines to the rectangle corners.

3. Cut along the drawn lines inside the rectangle.

4. Along the perimeter of the rectangle, fold the cut fabric edges toward the wrong side and press to create the window opening. The fold should be along the drawn lines of the initial rectangle.

Tip!

If you don't have a zipper foot handy, place the edge of a standard presser foot along the zipper teeth, and move the needle position to the left until it is ⅛" (3.2mm) from the edge of the fabric.

5. Center the window opening over the zipper tape, then stitch in place close to the folded edges of the fabric.

Fasteners

Other than the classic zipper, snaps, hook and eye, frog closures, and hook and loop tape are other great ways to hold a garment together. Each of these options offer its own unique function and flair.

Grommet or Eyelet

A grommet or eyelet is a small metal ring that is inserted into fabric to reinforce a hole. They are used everywhere from shoelace or drawstring openings to the corners of tarps or banners.

1. To install a grommet or eyelet, cut or punch a hole in the fabric the appropriate size for the grommet or eyelet being used. This measurement will generally be noted with the packaging instructions.

2. There are two sides or ends of a grommet or eyelet. The male end, which has a higher center section, and a female end, which is flatter in the center.

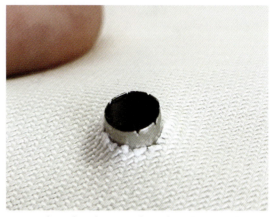

3. From the right side, insert the male end into the fabric hole opening.

Closures / Fasteners

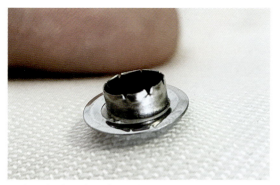

4. Place the female end over the male end.

5. Using a pair of grommet or eyelet pliers, squeeze the ends together. This will flatten the raised male end over the female end and secure them together over the fabric opening.

Snaps

A snap is two discs of either metal or plastic that fasten together to hold layers of fabric. They are commonly found on clothing but can also be found on bags or other home décor projects like pillows. Like grommets and eyelets, snaps can require a specific tool to secure them in place. Snaps have multiple parts; a ball, a socket, and a back that attaches to both the ball and socket. Snap backs can either be open rings or solid backs of plastic, metal, or other decorative material like pearl.

1. At the desired snap location, cut or punch the size of hole in the fabric as instructed on the package, then place the ball half of the snap on one side of the fabric and a snap back on the other.

2. Squeeze the two pieces together using a pair of snap pliers. The snap pliers will have a hole opening that allows the ball of the snap to go in so that it is not smashed or damaged by the pliers.

3. Directly across from the ball half of the snap on the second piece of fabric, place the socket half of the snap on one side of the fabric and a snap back on the other. Squeeze the two pieces together.

Tip!

Some snaps don't require you to punch or cut a hole in fabric first; rather, they have sharp points that simply pierce through the fabric. However, these are still clamped together on either side of a fabric like the snaps just mentioned.

Tip!

Snaps can also come in sew-in varieties. Rather than having a back that gets placed with either half of the snap, sew-in snaps have several openings around the perimeter of the snap halves that allow them to be sewn to secure to the fabric with thread.

Closures / Fasteners

Hook and Eye

A hook-and-eye closure is a small clasp that secures two pieces of fabric together. It consists of a bent piece of metal or plastic called a hook and a small loop of metal or plastic called the eye. Both pieces have small openings on either side that allow them to be sewn in place.

1. Bring a needle with a knotted length of thread up through the fabric and one opening of the eye. Pass the needle over the eye opening, then take the needle back down through the fabric. Repeat with another stitch, then repeat again to take several stitches through the remaining opening of the eye.

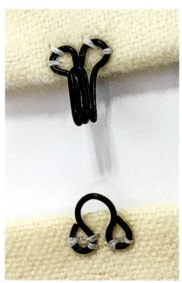

2. Repeat the same process to attach the hook to a second piece of fabric, securing it with several stitches around both openings of the hook.

Hook-and-eye closures can either be attached at the edges of fabric to hold them together, like at the upper edge of a skirt waistband above a zipper, or further in along a fabric edge where two layers of fabric need to be held together on top of one another, like on a bra closure.

Frog

A frog closure is a decorative closure that functions like a hook and eye. Rather than being made from metal or plastic, a frog closure is made from a cord. It has a small knot on one side and loop on the other. Frog closures are sewn in place at the edges of fabric directly across from one another. The loop of one side is passed around the knot of the other side to secure the closure and hold the fabric together.

Hook-and-Loop Tape

Hook-and-loop tape, commonly referred to as VELCRO®, is a closure that can be pushed together to secure and then easily pulled back apart. Hook-and-loop tape has two halves. One half has "hooks," or small, stiff pieces of plastic or other similar material. The other half is soft, fuzzy and has lots of little "loops" of nylon, polyester, or another similar material.

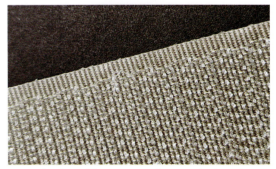

Hook-and-loop tape can either be sewn in place or adhered with an adhesive back that comes on the tape. To secure hook-and-loop tape with the adhesive back, simply remove the paper backing from the tape and stick in place at the desired location.

To sew hook-and-loop tape in place, stitch along the outer perimeter close to the edge.

Closures / Fasteners

Buttons

Buttons, used in conjunction with buttonholes, hold two layers of fabric together. Buttons can come in a variety of sizes, shapes, colors, materials, and types. The main types of buttons are two- and four-hole buttons, which are flat buttons with either two or four holes in the center, and shank buttons, which are solid on the right side and have a small loop or shank on the back that allows them to be sewn in place.

Buttons come in many shapes, sizes, materials, and colors!

Shank buttons are solid on the right side and have a shank on the back that allows them to be sewn in place.

Trick!

You can quickly sew two-hole buttons onto fabric by folding the fabric in half before you stitch! Place the folded edge of fabric over one of the buttonhole openings, leaving the other one open. Take a knotted length of thread down through the fabric and covered buttonhole, then bring it back up through the open one. Repeat several times, tie a knot, and your button is secure!

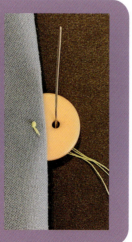

Hack!

Use an ice cube tray with a lid to sort and store buttons.

Buttonholes

A buttonhole is a small opening in fabric, generally reinforced with either hand or machine stitching, that allows a button to pass through it. Buttonholes can either be rectangular, have rounded ends, or have a small keyhole shape on one end.

Tip!

In general, vertical buttonholes should be used in areas of a garment where there is minimal stress, for example the front button band of a looser fitting shirt or blouse. Horizontal buttonholes can be used where there might be stress on the button, for example, the top button on a pair of jeans or the neckband of a collar. With a horizontal buttonhole, there is less of a risk of the button slipping out of the buttonhole.

A rectangular buttonhole is one of the most used and is considered a standard buttonhole. It is best sewn on medium to heavyweight fabrics.

An oval or rounded buttonhole has a rounded top and bottom. It is generally used on lighter-weight or more delicate fabrics.

A keyhole buttonhole has a wider opening on one end. It is generally used on heavier-weight or thicker fabrics in combination with a shank button.

Tip!
Explore your machine! Many machines have the capability of doing decorative buttonholes as well.

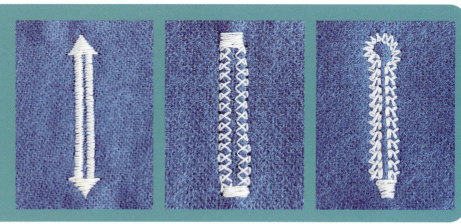

Rectangular Bound Buttonhole

A bound buttonhole has the raw edges of the buttonhole encased in fabric and is a professional-looking way to finish larger buttonholes on jackets and other outerwear garments.

1. Begin by determining the size of the buttonhole. The height of the buttonhole will generally be between ⅜"–½" (1–1.2cm), while the width of the buttonhole can be determined by measuring the desired button and adding ⅜" (1cm). Draw a rectangle of this size on the wrong side of the garment fabric, then draw a horizontal line through the center.

2. From the fabric you want to use as the buttonhole flaps (which can be the same fabric as the garment, or a contrasting color), cut a 3" (7.6cm) square. Center this square over the drawn rectangle on the right side of the fabric and pin in place.

View from the wrong side.   *View from the right side.*

3. Sew the perimeter of the drawn rectangle.

4. On the wrong side, roughly ¼" (6.4mm) in from the edges, draw diagonal lines out to the four corners of the buttonhole.

5. Cut through all layers of fabric along the center horizontal line and the four diagonal lines out to the corners. Clip as close to the corners as possible without cutting through the stitching.

6. Pull the fabric from the 3" (7.6cm) square through the cut opening to the wrong side of the fabric. Press the square fabric flat. If there is any puckering around the edges, clip further into the corners.

Closures / Buttons

View from the wrong side.   *View from the right side.*

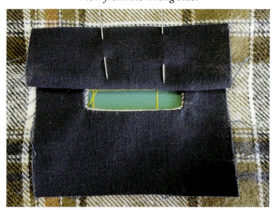 

7. Fold the top of the fabric square down, then back up on itself until the fold of the fabric is centered on the buttonhole opening. Pin in place.

8. Repeat to fold the bottom of the fabric square, then pin in place.

9. Fold back one edge of the pinned fabric square to reveal a small triangle of both fabrics. These triangles need to be stitched together and then to the fabric square.

10. With the garment right side up, fold all fabric out of the way to reveal the small triangle and the raw edges of the fabric square.

View from the wrong side. *View from the right side.*

11. Stitch across the triangle, backstitching at the beginning and end.

Triangular Bound Buttonhole

Bound buttonholes can also be made in a triangular shape.

1. Begin by determining the size of the buttonhole. The base of the triangle should be the diameter of the button, and the height should be at least ⅛" (3.2mm) taller than the button diameter.

3. At the desired buttonhole location and with the triangle pointing in the desired direction, place the marked square right sides together with the garment fabric. Pin in place, and then sew along the drawn triangle overlapping the beginning and ending of the stitching.

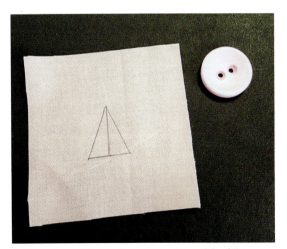 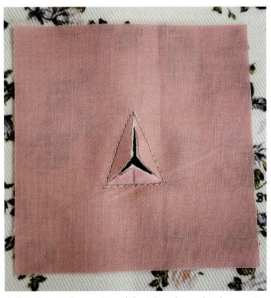

2. Cut a piece of fabric three times the width of the triangle base. For example, if the base of the triangle is 1 ¼" (3.2cm), cut a 3 ¾" (9.5cm) square of fabric. On the wrong side of the fabric square, center and draw the triangle.

4. Starting at the center of the triangle, make three cuts in the fabric going out toward the triangle points. Be careful not to cut through the stitching.

Closures / Buttons

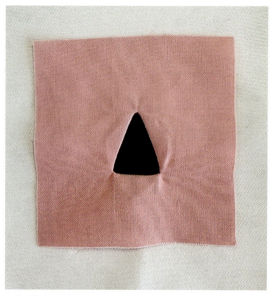

5. Push the fabric square through the triangle opening to the wrong side of the fabric and press flat.

6. Along one side of the triangle, fold the fabric square right sides together to cover the triangle, then fold it back down on itself with wrong sides together until the fold is at the center.

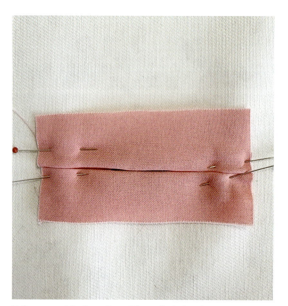

7. Repeat with the other side and pin in place.

8. Topstitch around the triangle approximately ⅛" (3.2mm) from the edge.

Invisible Buttonhole

An invisible buttonhole is a buttonhole opening made in fabric along a seam. This is a great option if you don't want to see the stitching of a standard buttonhole, or if you are working with a lightweight fabric where the stitching of a buttonhole would seem too bulky.

1. Start by cutting two strips of fabric that are approximately three times the diameter of the desired button in width and the length of the garment where the buttonholes are going, such as a shirt front. For example, if the button diameter is ½" (1.2cm), cut strips that are 1 ½" (3.8cm) wide by the length of the garment.

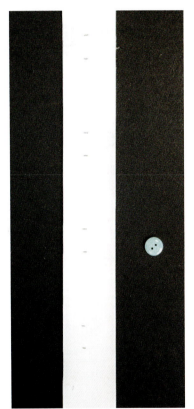

2. On the wrong side of one fabric strip, mark the buttonhole openings spaced the desired amount.

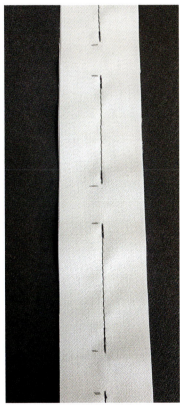

3. Align the fabric strips with right sides together and sew along the center of the strips, starting and stopping at the marked buttonhole openings. Backstitch at all beginnings and ends.

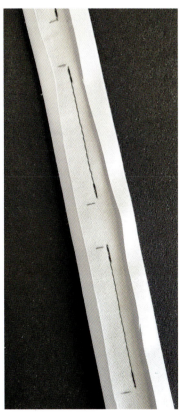

4. Along all raw edges, fold under and press ¼" (6.4mm) toward the wrong side.

Closures / Buttons

5. Fold the fabric along the stitching line so that the strips are aligned with wrong sides together. The stitching line and the buttonhole openings will be in the center.

6. Along one long side, align the folded edges and stitch together close to the edge.

7. Along the other long side, insert the garment edge. Stitch in place close to the edge on the side, upper, and lower edge.

Tip!
When sewing a top with buttons, men's shirts generally have buttons on the right, while women's shirts generally have buttons on the left.

Finishing Techniques

Not all projects have linings, which means there are many different scenarios where seams and fabric edges will be visible. Whether you are making a quilt and need to cover the raw edges of the top, batting, and backing fabric, or you're making a garment and need to keep the raw edges of the fabric from raveling and make them look professional, there's a finishing technique for every project.

Hems. 156

Binding 176

Seam Finishes. 186

Embellishments. 192

Hems

Hems are the finishing touch that can make or break a garment. Whether you're a beginner or an experienced sewer, mastering these techniques will elevate your sewing projects to a professional level.

Single-Fold Hem

A single-fold hem is one of the most basic ways to finish a fabric edge. To sew a single-fold hem, simply fold the fabric the desired amount toward the wrong side and stitch in place close to the fabric edge. The raw edge of the fabric will still be visible on the wrong side. Because of this, a single-fold hem is best used on fabrics that do not ravel, or done on a fabric edge that has been finished using a zigzag or overcast stitch.

Double-Fold Hem

A double-fold hem is a common way to finish a fabric edge and is used on everything from garments to accessories and home décor. To sew a double-fold hem, fold the fabric half of the desired hem amount toward the wrong side. Press in place and then fold the fabric the same amount again. Stitch the hem in place close to the upper folded edge.

Rolled Hem

A rolled hem is essentially a very narrow double-fold hem and is commonly used on lightweight fabric. To sew a rolled hem, start by installing a rolled hem foot on your machine. Insert the edge of the fabric all the way into the curve of the foot.

Sew using a standard straight stitch. As you sew, the foot will roll the fabric, and the hem will be stitched in place.

Hack!

If you don't have a rolled-hem foot, fold a thin piece of cardboard or cardstock at the desired hem width and tape it to your machine bed directly in front of the presser foot. Place your fabric into the folded edge of the cardstock, and sew a straight line. The fabric will be folded as it passes through the cardstock.

Finishing Techniques / Hems

Faced Hem

A faced hem is a way to finish a fabric edge and add a little weight to the hem.

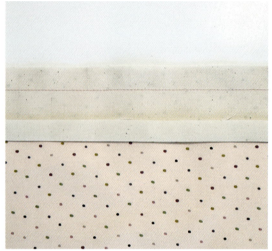

1. Cut a strip of fabric approximately 2 ½" (6.4cm) wide by the length of the fabric edge you want to finish. Fold under and press one edge by approximately ½" (1.2cm). With right sides together, sew the raw edge of the facing to the edge of the fabric using a ⅝" (1.6cm) seam allowance.

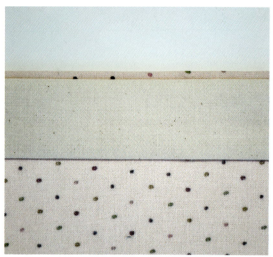

2. Press the seam allowances and facing to the wrong side. The amount you fold it toward the wrong side can depend on how much of the fabric you must work with. If this hem is on a garment, and folding it too far to the wrong side will make it too short, fold it so only a small amount of the garment fabric is seen on the wrong side. However, if you have more fabric to work with, you can fold it further.

3. Sew the facing in place along the upper pressed edge.

Blind Hem

A blind hem is another way to finish a fabric or garment edge so that there is not a visible line of stitching. Blind hems are commonly used on trousers or dress pants.

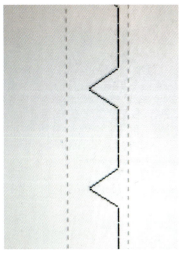

1. Install a blind-hem foot onto your machine and select the blind-hem stitch.

2. If your fabric ravels, finish the edge with a zigzag or overcast stitch, then fold the fabric the desired hem width amount toward the wrong side and press in place.

3. With right sides together, fold the fabric back down over itself until ¼" (6.4mm) of the zigzag-stitched edge is visible.

4. Place the fabric on the machine and align the folded edge of the fabric with the metal guide in the center of the foot.

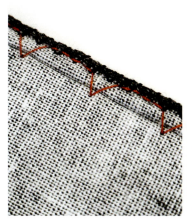

5. Sew using the blind-hem stitch. The stitch will place several straight stitches into the zigzag-finished edge of the fabric and then take a small stitch into the folded edge of the fabric.

6. Given how tiny the stitch into the folded fabric edge is, and especially if the fabric and thread color match, the stitches will be invisible on the right side of the fabric.

Side-Split Hem

A side-split hem is a technique that creates a split or vent opening in a hem but still has finished edges. Side split hems are commonly found on pants, shorts, or capris.

1. Determine how deep you want the split in the hem to be. It is common for a split to be anywhere from ½–⅔ of a hem allowance. For this example, the hem allowance will be 2" (5.1cm) and the split will be 1½" (3.8cm).

2. If desired, finish the raw edges of the garment fabric using either a zigzag or overcast stitch.

For another way to make a pant slit, see page 46!

3. Before the side seam of the garment is sewn, mark the hem fold line, then mark the split depth both above and below the fold line.

4. Align the fabric and sew the garment side seam using a standard seam allowance, leaving the seam open between the mark above and below the hem fold line. Backstitch at the beginning and end of the stitching lines.

5. Press the seam allowances above and below the unstitched area open.

6. With right sides together, fold the fabric along the hem fold line.

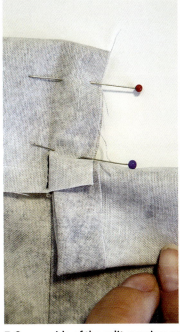  

7. On one side of the split opening, unfold the fabric and align the edges of the seam allowance. Pin in place and then stitch together from the folded edge of the fabric to the split opening.

8. Refold the seam allowance back on itself toward the wrong side and press.

9. Repeat on the other side of the split opening, then turn the hem right side out, fold along the hem fold line, and press in place.

Finishing Techniques / Hems

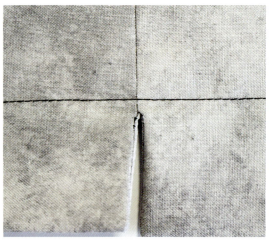

10. Stitch the hem in place.

> **Tip!**
> Keep your sewing speed consistent. Constantly speeding up or slowing down while sewing makes it hard to keep a straight line of stitching.

> **Tip!**
> If you want to add a side-split hem but don't want to see a line of stitching on the right side of the fabric, you can use fusible-hem tape or a blind-hem stitch.

Lace-Hem Tape

Lace-hem tape is a narrow strip of finished edge lace or ribbon.

Lace-hem tape adds a decorative touch to the wrong sides of garments and is also handy to use if you want the raw edge of the fabric to be finished but do not have enough fabric to sew a double-fold hem.

To use lace-hem tape, sew it close to the edge of a fabric. Fold the fabric edge with the lace-hem tape toward the wrong side the desired amount, then stitch in place along the upper edge of the tape.

Fusible-Hem Tape

Fusible-hem tape is a strip of double-sided fusible adhesive that can be used to hold a hem in place. It can be found in a variety of widths to accommodate whatever width of hem you are using, as well as a variety of weights to be used with everything from light to heavyweight fabric.

1. Fold and press the fabric toward the wrong side the desired hem width. Open the hem back up, then place a length of hem tape on the wrong side of the fabric next to the fold.

2. Refold the hem and press in place.

Tip!
Don't confuse hem tape with basting tape! Hem tape is a permanent adhesive, whereas basting tape will only temporarily hold your fabric together.

Finishing Techniques / Hems

Double-Fold Tape

Double-fold tape is a strip of fabric that has been folded in half twice and is used to finish a fabric edge. The fabric strip can be cut on the lengthwise grain if it is being used on a straight seam, or on the bias if it is being used on a curved edge.

1. Open the folds of the tape and pin one edge of the tape to the raw edge of the fabric, right sides together.

2. Sew in place along the fold line closest to the fabric edge.

3. Refold the tape along the fold lines and wrap the tape around to the other side of the fabric. The center fold of the tape will be along the raw edge of the fabric.

4. Secure the tape in place by sewing close to the folded edge of the tape on the unstitched side. *Note: If you don't want to see a line of stitching on the tape, you can secure it in place using an invisible hand stitch (see page 208).*

Tip!

The narrower side of pre-made double-fold bias tape should always be sewn to your project first.

Single-Fold Tape

Single-fold tape is a strip of fabric that has been folded once along both edges so that the edges meet in the middle. The fabric strip can be cut on the lengthwise grain if it is being used on a straight seam, or on the bias if it is being used on a curved edge.

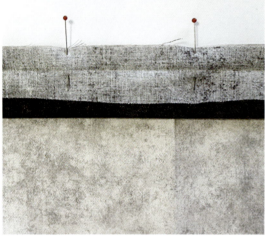

1. Open one of the folds of the tape and align the raw edge of the tape with the raw edge of the fabric, right sides together.

2. Sew in place along the fold line.

3. Fold the single-fold tape toward the wrong side of the fabric along the previous stitching line. Press in place.

4. Sew in place close to the upper folded edge of the tape.

Tip! Don't want to cut and press fabric strips for a faced hem? Buy premade single-fold tape instead!

French-Fold Tape

French-fold tape is a strip of fabric that has been folded in half with wrong sides together. The fabric strip can be cut on the lengthwise grain if it is being used on a straight seam, or on the bias if it is being used on a curved edge.

1. Align the raw edges of the tape with the raw edge of the fabric and pin in place.

2. Stitch in place approximately ¼" (6.4mm) from the edge.

3. Fold the tape around the raw edge of the fabric, and then sew in place close to the folded edge of the tape.

Easy Mitered Corner

1. Finish the fabric edges using a zigzag or overcast stitch.

2. With right sides together, fold the fabric in half diagonally so that the corner forms a point.

3. With the finished edges aligned, fold the point down until the folds form a 90° angle as shown.

4. Stitch so the stitch line is flush with the inner fold as shown, but not through it.

5. Turn right side out and push out the corner.

6. Press and, if desired, top stitch to secure close to the finished edges of the fabric.

Finishing Techniques / Hems

Mitered Corner: 90°

When attaching binding to the edge of a fabric, depending on the project you may need the binding to continue around a corner. Mitering the corner is a way to fold the fabric so that there is a 45° angled fold at the corner. For this example, French-fold tape will be shown.

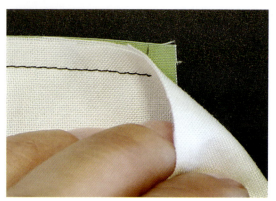

1. Start by sewing the tape to the raw edge of the fabric using a ¼" (6.4mm) seam allowance and ending the stitching ¼" (6.4mm) from the corner.

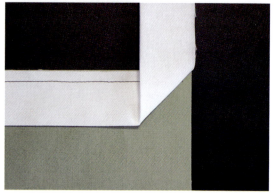

2. Fold the tape up onto itself at a 45° angle. The raw edge of the tape should be perfectly in line with the next edge of fabric the tape will be sewn to.

3. Fold the tape back down onto itself, aligning the raw edge of the tape with the raw edge of the fabric. The upper fold of the tape should align with the previous edge of the fabric.

4. Starting at the fabric edge, stitch the tape in place using a ¼" (6.4mm) seam allowance.

5. Fold the tape over the raw edge of the fabric.

6. At the corner, fold the tape down from one side first, then fold from the next side, ensuring that the folded edges of the tape meet in the center at a 45° angle.

7. Stitch the tape in place close to the folded edge.

Tip!
When attaching binding and mitering a corner, rather than just stopping the seam allowance width from the edge and turning, stitch off the corner of the fabric at a 45° angle. This will help ensure you get a straight 45° fold at the corner.

Mitered Corner: Double-Fold Hem

Mitered corners can be made on projects with a simple hemmed edge without needing to attach a binding tape.

1. To make the mitered corner using a ½" (1.2cm) double fold hem, measure and mark the ½" (1.2cm) fold lines on the wrong side of the fabric.

Finishing Techniques / Hems

2. Using a removable fabric marker, measure and mark the fold lines in the corner on the right side of the fabric.

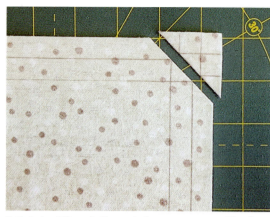

3. Cut at a 45° angle through the square created by the marked fold lines.

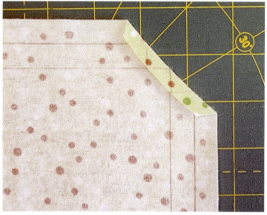

4. Fold the fabric along the cut edge toward the wrong side until the marked fold lines align, then press.

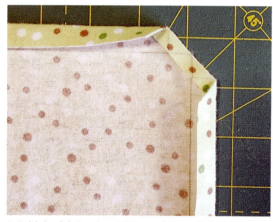

5. Fold the fabric edges ½" (1.2cm) toward the wrong side and press.

6. Fold the fabric another ½" toward the wrong side and press to create the mitered corner.

Trick!

When sewing corners on bulkier fabrics, it is important to always clip the corners before tuning the project right side out. If you are struggling to get crisp corners even after clipping at the standard 45° angle, consider clipping twice.

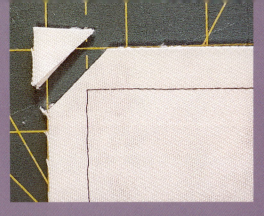

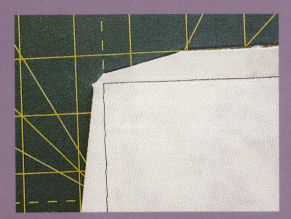

Once the first clip is done, clip again on each side at a roughly 30° angle to reduce the bulk in the corner even more, and allow for the fabric to lay flatter and your corners to have a nice 90° angle. Even with a double clip, perfect corners when turning thick fabrics right side out can still be difficult simply because there is a lot of bulk. One way to get better points is to take a diagonal stitch in the corner.

1. To do this, start by sewing the seam along one fabric edge as normal and stop one stitch from the corner with the needle down. Pivot the fabric 45°, take one stitch, then stop with the needle down. Again, pivot the fabric 45° and continue stitching down the next side of fabric.

2. Trim the seam allowances, double-clip the corners, then turn the fabric right side out and push out the corner point.

Finishing Techniques / Hems

Mitered Corner: Borders

Mitered corners can also be made on the outer edge of a fabric and still have a raw edge that needs to be finished, like if you are adding a border to a project.

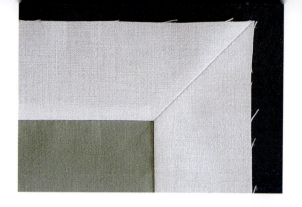

1. Cut border strips of fabric longer than the center fabric by twice the border strip width, plus 1" (2.5cm). For example, if the border strip is 2" (5.1cm) wide, the strip length should be the center fabric width plus (2" x 2") + 1", or 5" [(2 x 5.1cm) + 2.5cm, or 12.7cm]. This will give you a little extra to trim off after the strips are sewn in place. With right sides together, center the border strip on the fabric so that there are equal amounts of overhang on both sides. Sew using a ¼" (6.4mm) seam allowance starting and stopping the stitching ¼" (6.4mm) from the edge.

2. Fold the border strip away from the center fabric, then repeat to attach another border strip to the next side of the center fabric, again starting and stopping the stitching ¼" (6.4mm) from the edge.

3. Fold the center fabric in half, aligning the raw edges of the border strips.

4. Using a square ruler with a 45° line on it, align the 45° line of the ruler with the raw edge of the border strips. The edge of the ruler will align with the folded edge of the center fabric. Draw a line on the border strips along the edge of the ruler.

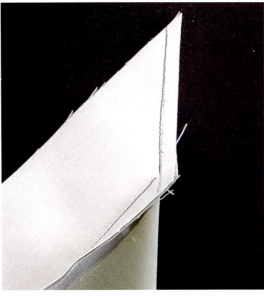

5. Sew on the drawn line, then trim the remaining excess fabric ¼" (6.4mm) from the stitching.

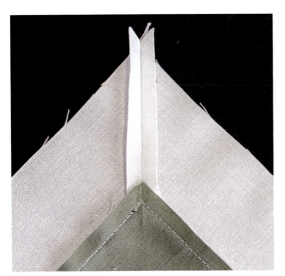

6. Open and press the seam allowances open and the center fabric toward the border strips, then clip off the little triangles of fabric that extend beyond the border strips.

Tip!
Always stop with the needle down when turning a corner.

Binding

Binding adds a polished edge to your sewing projects, providing both durability and aesthetic appeal. Whether you're finishing quilts, garments, or accessories, these techniques will help you achieve clean, professional edges every time.

Continuous Bias Binding

Depending on the size of project you may be finishing with bias binding, you may not be able to do it with one strip of fabric and will need to attach several strips together to get the needed length. Since bias binding is cut on the bias, it leaves you with longer strips cut from the center of a piece of fabric that slowly get shorter as you work your way across the fabric. Rather than sewing together many small strips of fabric to get one length, you can make continuous bias binding.

1. Start with a square of fabric that is cut on the straight of grain. (See page 244 for how to find the straight of grain.) Cut the square in half diagonally.

2. Position the fabric triangles right sides together so that one straight edge is aligned, and the long bias edges are toward the center. Offset the aligned edges by ¼" (6.4mm). Sew in place using a ¼" (6.4mm) seam allowance.

3. Press the seam allowance open, then draw parallel lines on the wrong side of the fabric spaced the desired bias tape-width apart.

 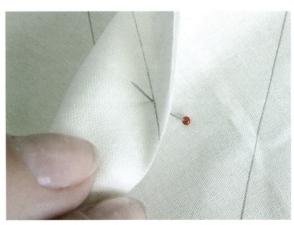

4. Align the short raw ends of the fabric with right sides together, offsetting the drawn lines by one. The lines should be aligned ¼" (6.4mm) from the edge, since that is the seam allowance. The easiest way to do this is to place a straight pin through the fabric on the line ¼" (6.4mm) from the edge. The pin should come out through the other fabric ¼" (6.4mm) from the edge directly on the line.

Finishing Techniques / Binding

5. Pin in place and then stitch using a ¼" (6.4mm) seam allowance.

6. Cut along the drawn lines. Because the lines were offset by one, you will continue cutting around the stitched tube of fabric, resulting in one long strip of bias binding.

Calculate Continuous Bias Binding

If you are using the previous method of creating continuous bias binding using a square of fabric and have a specific project in mind, there's a quick way to determine the size of square you will need to start with to get enough continuous bias binding.

Start by measuring the perimeter of your project to get the total length of binding needed. Multiply this number by the binding strip width. For example, if you need 150" (381cm) of binding, and the binding strip will be cut at 2" (5.1cm) wide, multiply 150 x 2 for a total of 300" (762cm).

Next, take the square root of this number. If the number is not a whole number, round up to the nearest whole number. For example, the square root of 300 is 17.32. Round this up to 18. This means you would use the method of creating continuous bias binding starting with an 18" (45.72cm) square.

Tip!

You can turn a narrow tube right side out using ribbon, yarn, or other string.

1. Lay the ribbon on the right side of the fabric, fold the fabric in half, and stitch the long side and one short side. Ensure that the ribbon is stitched into the seam of the short side.

2. Pull on the other end of the ribbon to turn the tube right side out.

Tip!

Turn a narrow tube right side out using a straw and a chopstick!

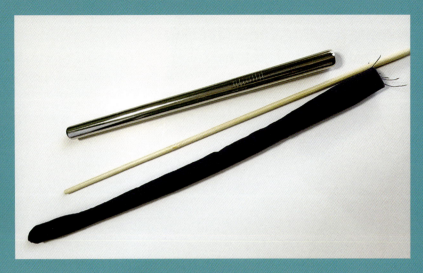

1. Stitch both long sides and one short end of the tube.

2. Insert the straw into the remaining open short end of the tube and push it all the way to the other (stitched) end.

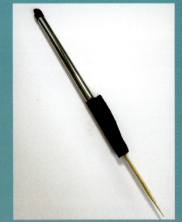

3. Place the chopstick on the stitched end and then push it down the center of the straw to turn the tube right side out.

Finishing Techniques / Binding

Joining Binding Ends: Overlap

Depending on your project, there may come a point where you need to join the end of a binding strip with the beginning. An easy way to do this is to just overlap the ends. For this example, French-fold tape will be shown.

1. Begin sewing the binding to the project roughly 3" (7.6cm) from the edge of the binding, leaving the beginning unstitched.

2. As you work your way around the project with the binding, stop stitching 4–5" (10.2–12.7cm) from the beginning.

3. Along the short raw edge of the beginning of the binding, fold and press the fabric ¼" (6.4mm) toward the wrong side.

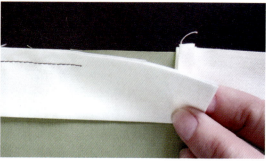

4. Overlap the binding end over the folded binding beginning by approximately ½" (1.2cm) and trim away the remainder.

5. Place the unfinished edge of the binding inside the folded edge, then finish stitching the remainder of the binding to the raw edge of the project, securing the overlapped fabric.

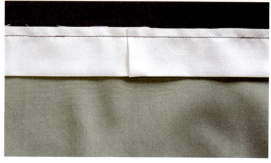

6. Fold the binding over the raw edge, keeping the fabric overlapped. Pin and stitch in place.

Tip!

Never sew over a pin! Doing so runs the risk of hitting the pin with the needle. This could bend or break both the needle or the pin, or even throw the timing off on your machine. If you struggle to take pins out of the fabric as you sew up to them, try pinning with the pin perpendicular to the fabric edge, rather than parallel. This makes the head of the pin easier to grab.

Joining Binding Ends: Diagonal

Another way to join binding ends is to do so with a diagonal seam. This eliminates the bulk of overlapped fabric as well as any bulk from seam allowances being directly on top of one another with a straight seam. For this example, French-fold tape will be shown.

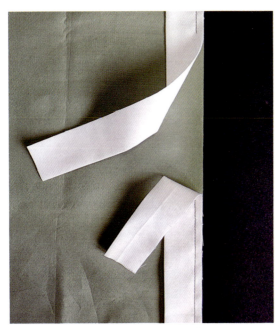

1. Attach the binding to the perimeter of the project, leaving tails of binding at the beginning and end and an opening of approximately 6" (15.2cm) unstitched between the beginning and end.

2. Lay the end of the binding flat along the unstitched edge of the project. Overlap the binding beginning over the end by the measurement of the binding width, then trim the remaining. For example, if the binding strips were cut at 2 ½" (6.4cm) wide, overlap the binding beginning over the end by 2 ½" (6.4cm) and trim the remainder.

3. Open both binding ends and align them with right sides together at a 90° angle. The center fabric will need to be folded or bunched up a bit to make this happen.

4. Draw a diagonal line from the outer corner of one strip to the outer corner of the other, then sew along the drawn line.

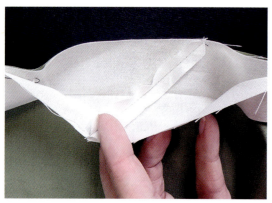

5. Trim the excess fabric at a ¼" (6.4mm) seam allowance, then press the seam allowance open.

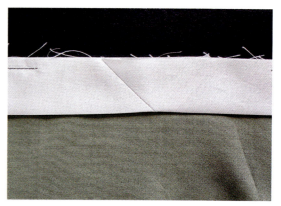

6. Lay the binding flat along the project edge, then refold in half.

7. Stitch the remainder of the binding in place.

Tip!

When joining strips of fabric together to make binding, it is best to sew them using a diagonal seam. This will reduce bulk when the binding is folded in half and wrapped around the edge of a project.

Flange Binding

A flange binding is a way to create a two-toned binding, or the look of having an additional strip of fabric between the binding and the project.

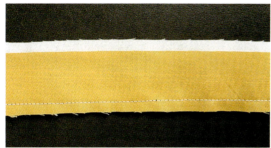

1. Start by cutting strips from two coordinating colors of fabric. The strip cut from the fabric color you want the flange to be will need to be ¼" (6.4mm) wider that the fabric you cut for the binding strip, with both pieces equaling the desired binding width once they are sewn together using a ¼" (6.4mm) seam allowance. For example, if you want the total binding width to be 2 ½" (6.4cm), the flange strip would be cut at 1⅝" (4.13cm) and the binding strip would be cut at 1⅜" (3.49cm). With right sides together, sew the strips and then press the seam allowance toward the binding strip.

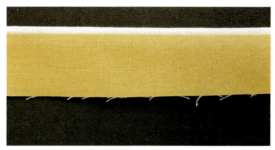

2. With wrong sides together, press the binding in half.

3. To attach a flange binding to a project, align the binding with the raw edge on the wrong side of the project with the flange strip down against the fabric.

4. Wrap the binding around the fabric edge and secure in place by stitching in the seamline between the binding and flange strips using either a coordinating or contrasting thread.

Finishing Techniques / Binding

Binding from Backing

If the project you are making has layers of fabric, like a quilt, table runner, or placemat, you can use the backing fabric as the binding, wrapping it around the raw edges to finish them.

1. Start by trimming the backing fabric twice the binding width measurement around the perimeter of the project. For example, if you want an approximately ½" (1.2cm) finished binding, trim the backing fabric 1" (2.5cm) away from the top fabric. Depending on the thickness of the project, the finished binding might end up slightly thinner. Trim the batting flush with the top layer of fabric.

2. Starting along one side, fold the raw edge of the backing fabric until it aligns with the raw edge of the top fabric.

3. Fold in half again so that the backing fabric wraps around the raw edge of the top fabric, then pin in place.

4. Fold the backing fabric in this manner along the entire edge of the project until you reach a corner. At the corner, fold the fabric in half and then in half again as if it were being wrapped around the project.

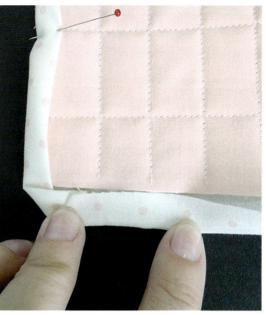

5. Starting along the next edge of the fabric, fold the folded end of the backing fabric at a 45° angle until it aligns with the raw edge of the project.

6. Fold the fabric in half until the raw edge of the backing fabric aligns with the raw edge of the top fabric.

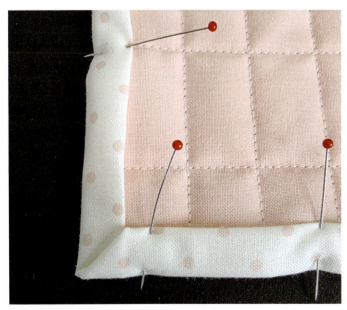

8. Repeat at all corners and then stitch in place close to the folded edge of the backing fabric.

7. Fold in half again so that the backing fabric wraps around the raw edge of the top fabric.

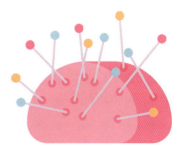

Finishing Techniques / Binding **185**

Seam Finishes

Seam finishes are essential for creating durable and polished garments. In this section, we'll cover various techniques to finish seams, including zigzag, welt, and French seams. These methods will help prevent fraying and ensure your projects look as good on the inside as they do on the outside.

Flat-Felled Seam

A flat-felled seam is a common way to finish seam allowances on garments. This method hides all fabric raw edges and makes the wrong side of a garment look finished and professional.

1. Sew the seam with a standard ⅝" (1.6cm) seam allowance, then trim one side of the seam allowance by half.

2. With the seam open, fold the untrimmed seam allowance in half over the trimmed half until the raw edge aligns with the stitching line.

Trick!

When pinning a flat-felled seam on a sleeve that has been set in, slide a long quilting ruler down the sleeve to keep the layers of the sleeve apart so that you only pin through one layer.

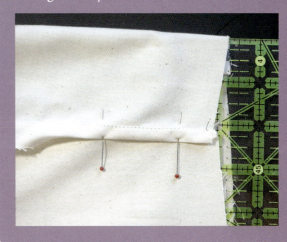

3. Lay the folded seam allowance flat against the fabric and pin in place.

Tip!

Use an Add a Quarter ruler to easily trim seam allowances to ¼" (6.4mm) when flat felling a seam. The groove of the ruler will "lock" against the seam. Trimming along the edge of the ruler will leave the seam allowance at exactly ¼" (6.4mm).

4. Edgestitch in place close to the fold.

Finishing Techniques / Seam Finishes

French Seam

French seams are commonly used in garment construction and are a way to finish a seam as a garment is being sewn.

1. Start by aligning the fabric wrong sides together and sew the seam using a ⅜" (1cm) seam allowance.

2. Trim the seam allowance to approximately ⅛" (3.2mm).

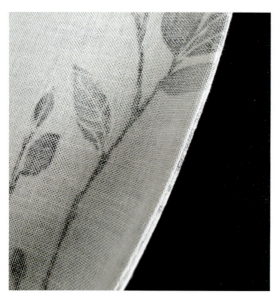

3. Refold the fabric with right sides together, ensuring that the previous seam allowance is right along the folded edge.

4. Stitch using a ¼" (6.4mm) seam allowance. This completes the standard ⅝" (1.6cm) seam allowance and finishes the seam at the same time.

Hong Kong Seam

A Hong Kong seam is pressed open, then each raw edge of the seam allowance is finished with a single-fold tape. The tape can be either a coordinating or contrasting color. The fabric strip for the tape can be cut on the lengthwise grain if it is being used on a straight seam, or on the bias if it is being used on a curved edge.

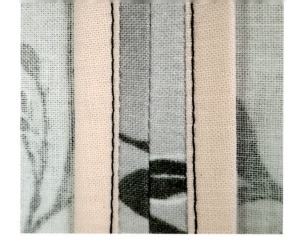

1. Start by sewing the seam and pressing it open.

2. Next, open a strip of single-fold tape and sew it to one side of the seam allowance with right sides together, stitching in the fold line.

3. Fold the tape over the seam allowance to the wrong side. From the right side, stitch through the seam allowance and single fold tape only, approximately ⅛" (3.2mm) from the edge of the tape.

4. Repeat to sew a strip of single-fold tape to the remaining side of the seam allowance, then repress the seam allowance open.

Finishing Techniques / Seam Finishes

Zigzag Seam

A zigzag seam is a quick and easy way to keep the raw edges of a seam allowance from raveling. Simply run a line of zigzag stitches over the edge of the seam allowance. The left-hand swing of the needle will take a stitch into the fabric while the right-hand swing will go off the edge of the fabric. A similar effect can be created using an overcast stitch as well.

Welt Seam

A welt seam is sometimes referred to as a faux or mock flat-felled seam because it looks like a flat-felled seam on the right side of the fabric. It is a good seam finish to do on heavier-weight or bulky fabrics.

1. Start by sewing the seam and finishing the seam allowance edges using a zigzag or overcast stitch.

2. Press the seam allowance to one side, then, from the right side, topstitch through the fabric and seam allowances roughly ¼" (6.4mm) from the seam.

Lapped Seam

A lapped seam is a seam made by simply placing one side of the fabric over the other and sewing them together. This type of seam is best used on fabrics that do not fray or ravel.

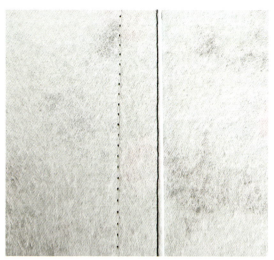

2. Flip the fabric over, then edgestitch close to the remaining fabric edge.

1. With right sides up, overlap the edges of two pieces of fabric. Edgestitch close to the fabric edge on the top.

Tip!

Don't watch the needle while you sew! Rather than watching the needle, watch the edge of your fabric toward the front of your presser foot. Doing this will allow you to make any adjustments to your fabric to keep the desired seam allowance before the fabric is at the needle and helps you keep a straighter line of stitching.

Finishing Techniques / Seam Finishes

Embellishments

Embellishments add unique flair and personality to your sewing projects. The embellishments here, including topstitching, scallops, and various piping methods, will help you transform your projects into one-of-a-kind masterpieces.

Topstitching

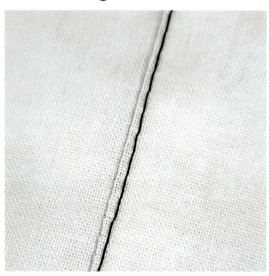

Topstitching is a technique where a line of stitches with an elongated stitch length is made close to the edge of a seam. Topstitching can be both functional and decorative. It can help strengthen a seam by adding an additional row of stitching, and it can help secure seam allowances to one side or the other. Decorative topstitching is often done in a contrasting thread color and can be done in one or multiple lines.

Stay Stitching

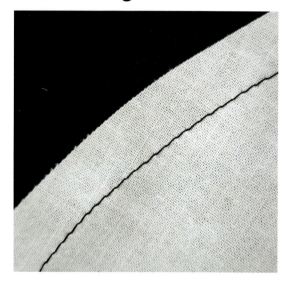

Stay stitching is a line of stitching done along a cut edge of fabric to help stabilize it during construction. It is more common to see stay stitching done along curved edges, as the bias of fabric is where there is the most stretch.

Understitching

Understitching is the technique of sewing a facing or lining together with the seam allowance where it is attached to a garment. The stitching should be very close to the seam allowance and is meant to keep the lining or facing from rolling to the outside of a garment.

> ### Trick!
> If you've ever struggled to start a seam at the edge of a fabric, either because you can't get the fabric to feed through the machine, or the fabric gets pushed down into the throat plate area of the machine, try starting the seam on a scrap piece of fabric first. This will allow you to stitch off the scrap fabric right onto your project fabric. The scrap fabric can then be cut away after and used over and over.

Prairie Points

Prairie points are small, folded triangles typically added to the seams of projects like quilts, table runners, and placemats as embellishments.

1. To make prairie points, cut squares of fabric. The squares can be cut at any size, making this a great use of scrap fabric. The larger the starting square, the larger the finished prairie point. For this example, 3" (7.6cm) squares will be used.

2. With wrong sides together, fold the square in half diagonally and press.

3. Fold the triangle in half again and press. Repeat with all your squares.

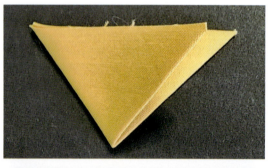

4. Lay out the first prairie point with the folded edge on the left. Open the other side of the point and tuck the folded edge of the next point inside. Overlap the points by approximately ½" (1.2cm), and then pin in place.

5. Repeat with the remaining points, then baste the row of points together approximately ⅛" (3.2mm) from the lower raw edge. The points are now ready to be added to a project.

6. To do this, simply layer the raw edge of the points along the raw edge of a project fabric. Layer another fabric on top with right sides together and stitch using a ¼" (6.4mm) seam allowance.

Tip!

If you find it hard to pre-pin a long row of points and then bring them to your machine, you can add the points at the machine as you sew.

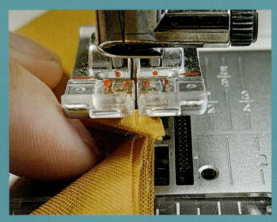

1. Start by marking the depth that you want the points to overlap with a pin, and then baste up to that pin.

2. Remove the pin, open the layers of the point, insert the next point, and then continue stitching.

Finishing Techniques / Embellishments

Scallops

Another edging embellishment that can be added to the seams of a project is a scallop. A scallop is a finished semi-circle or curved edge.

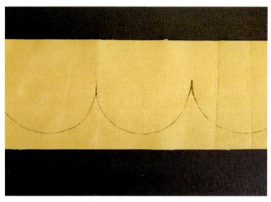

1. Cut two strips of fabric approximately ¾" (1.9cm) taller than you want the final scallop to be. Next, using a scallop template, or creating your own using template plastic or a piece of cardstock, trace the scallop shapes onto the wrong side of one of the fabric strips ¼" (6.4mm) from the upper edge.

2. Align the strips with right sides together, then stitch along the drawn lines. Trim the seam allowance to ¼" (6.4mm) and then clip small notches along the curves.

Tip!
Quickly notch the curved edges with pinking shears!

3. In the valleys between each scallop, clip up to the stitching line.

4. Turn right side out and press. The scallops are now ready to be added to a project.

Piping

Piping is narrow cording with a strip of fabric folded around it. It can be added to seams as a decorative trim and is used everywhere from garments to home décor and upholstery. Piping can be purchased premade, or you can make your own.

1. Start with a length of cord anywhere from ⅛–¼" (3.2–6.4mm) in diameter. Narrower cording is more commonly used in garments, while thicker cording is used in home décor and upholstery. Cut a strip of fabric on the bias that is approximately six times the diameter of the cord. For example, if the cord is ¼" (6.4mm), cut the strip of fabric at 1 ½" (3.8cm).

2. Place the cording in the center of the fabric strip against the wrong side. Fold the fabric in half, then stitch along the edge of the cording using a zipper foot. You want the stitching to be approximately ¹⁄₁₆" (1.6mm) away from the cording. This will allow you to stitch closer to the cording when installing the piping into a project, keeping the initial line of stitching hidden.

3. To install piping into a project, sandwich the piping between two layers of fabric with the fabric layers right sides together.

Finishing Techniques / Embellishments

4. If you are making a project where the seam allowance may not matter as much, simply align the project fabric raw edges with the piping fabric raw edges. Install a piping foot onto the machine, or continue using the zipper foot, and sew the fabric layers together as close to the cording as possible without stitching into the cording itself.

If you are adding piping into a garment where you need to maintain a ⅝" (1.6cm) seam allowance, position the piping so that the edge of the cording is along the seam line of the garment fabric and baste or pin in place. Place the other garment fabric on top of the piping with right sides together and then stitch using a ⅝" (1.6cm) seam allowance.

Piping on Curves

Because the strip of fabric to make piping is cut on the bias, if you have a curved edge in your project, you can simply follow along the fabric edge with the piping. The more curved a project is, you may want to baste the piping to one layer of fabric first before adding the second fabric. This will help keep the piping smooth around the curves. Do this by stitching right in the same line of stitching that secured the fabric around the cord.

Piping on Corners

If your project requires you to turn a corner, follow these steps.

1. End the stitches a seam allowance width away from the corner.

2. At the end of the stitching, clip the piping fabric up to approximately 1/16" (1.6mm) away from the stitching of the piping.

3. Bend the piping at the corner, then position it along the next fabric edge and pin in place.

4. Reposition the project fabric with right sides together over the piping and stitch along the next edge. Double clip the corners, then turn right side out and press. (See page 173 for how to double clip corners.)

Finishing Techniques / Embellishments

Joining Piping Ends

Whether you've gone around a curve or turned several corners, or you simply ran out of piping and need to add more, you may be to a point where you need to join two ends of piping together.

1. At the end of the piping, leave approximately 2" (5.1cm) unstitched.

2. Unpick the stitches along the first 1½" (3.8cm). Open the fabric of the piping and trim just the cording by 1" (2.5cm).

3. Fold and press the fabric edge ¼" (6.4mm) toward the wrong side.

4. Cut the fabric and cord flush with one another on the next piece of piping, then position the new piping inside the folded fabric end of the previous piping, ensuring that the two cut cord ends are right against one another.

5. Refold the fabric and align the raw edges of the piping and the project. Stitch the remainder of the piping in place.

Rickrack

Rickrack is a flat piece of decorative trim shaped in various widths of zigzags. It can be added to a seam as a decorative edge, or stitched onto the surface of a fabric as an embellishment.

1. Position the center of the rickrack along the seam allowance line of a piece of fabric and pin in place.

2. Position a second piece of fabric right sides together with the first, and stitch the fabric layers using the desired seam allowance. Turn the fabrics right side out and press the fabric away from the rickrack.

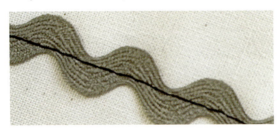

To attach rickrack to the surface of a fabric as an embellishment, simply sew the rickrack in place along the center. Use either a coordinating or contrasting thread, depending on the desired look.

Trick!

Another fun option when adding rickrack to the surface of a fabric is to twist two lengths together. Do this by selecting two lengths of trim that are the same zigzag width.

1. Starting at one end, pin the trim together to secure, then bring the length of trim on the left side over the right.

2. Continue passing the trim on the left over the right until you reach the end of the rickrack. Stitch the twisted rickrack to the surface of a fabric down the center to secure in place.

Finishing Techniques / Embellishments

Hand Sewing

Even if you sew most of your garments and other projects on a sewing machine, there will come a time when you need to sew something by hand. This could be because you want to finish a seam on a bag lining so that it is invisible, or you simply need to sew on a button. Either way, knowing some hand-sewing stitches is bound to come in handy!

How to Tie a Knot 204

Hand Sewing 206

How to Tie a Knot

Before you do any kind of hand sewing or embroidery, you need to add a knot at the end of the thread to secure it from pulling through the fabric.

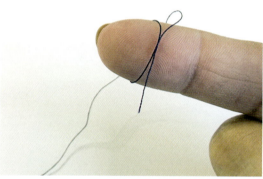

1. One of the easiest ways to do this is to start by wrapping the end of the thread around your pointer finger. This can be done with either a single or double strand of thread.

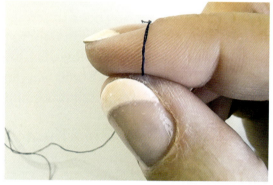

2. Rub your pointer finger against your thumb to roll the threads together.

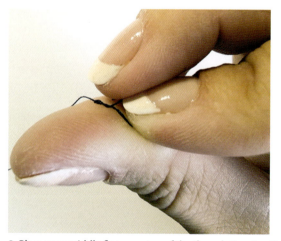

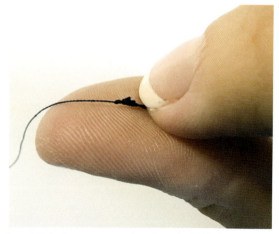

3. Place your middle finger on top of the thread. Keeping the thread tight between your thumb and middle finger, pull the rolled threads down toward the end of the thread until they pull tight into a knot.

Trick!

There are times when knots are harder to hide than others so, the next time you run into one of those cases, use this no-knot sewing trick!

1. Take a length of thread and thread both ends through the eye of the needle. There will be two raw ends on one side of the needle and a loop on the other.

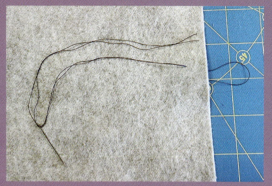

2. Take the first stitch where needed and pull the thread through until there is a small loop of thread left on the wrong side of the fabric.

3. Take a small stitch, approximately 1/16" (1.6mm) away from where the needle came out, and pull the thread back through to the wrong side of the fabric, being careful to keep the thread loop on the wrong side of the fabric.

4. Flip your work over, then pass the needle through the thread loop and pull tight.

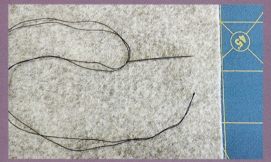

5. The thread is now secured and you have nothing more than a tiny stitch on the wrong side of the fabric.

Hand Sewing / How to Tie a Knot

Hand-Sewing Stitches

Note that all stitches will be shown using a double strand of thread, but can be done with a single strand as well.

Running Stitch

A running stitch is one of the most basic and commonly used hand-sewing stitches.

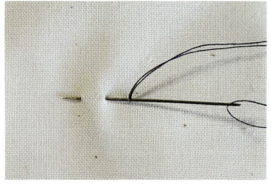

1. Bring the needle through the fabric from the wrong side to hide the knot. Take the needle down through the fabric to the wrong side the desired stitch length away, then bring it back up through to the right side of the fabric at the same stitch length.

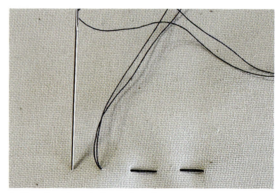

2. Keeping the stitch spacing the same, repeat to take the needle back down through the fabric to the wrong side, and then back up through to the right.

Tip!

To make a running stitch even faster, you can load several stitches onto the needle at the same time before pulling the needle through to complete the stitches.

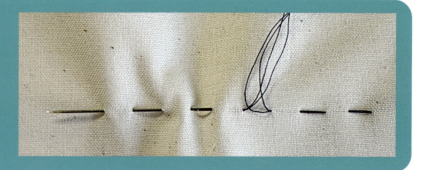

Basting Stitch

A basting stitch is essentially a really long running stitch. It is meant to temporarily hold layers of fabric together and is typically removed once the pieces have been secured using another stitch.

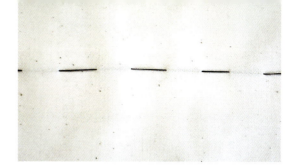

Backstitch

A backstitch is a common construction stitch when hand sewing, because it is very strong and secure.

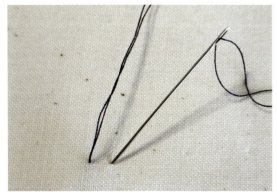

1. Bring the needle through the fabric from the wrong side to hide the knot. Take the needle down through the fabric the desired stitch length behind where the thread is coming up through the fabric.

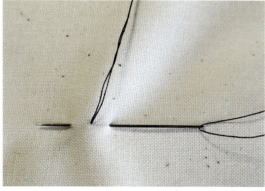

2. Bring the needle up through the fabric the same stitch length in front of where the thread is coming up through the fabric.

3. Take the needle back down through the fabric at the same point where the thread first came through the fabric.

4. Repeat to bring the needle up through the fabric the same stitch length in front of the previous stitch, then take the needle back down through the fabric at the end of the previous stitch.

Hand Sewing / Hand-Sewing Stitches

Ladder Stitch

A ladder stitch, also known as an invisible hand stitch, is a great stitch to use when you need to secure pieces of fabric together but don't want the stitching to be visible, like the lining of a bag or the stuffing opening of a pillow.

1. Bring the needle through the fabric from the wrong side in the pressed crease of a seam allowance.

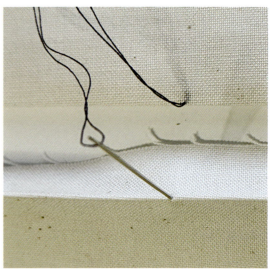

2. Take the needle down through the second piece of fabric in the pressed crease of the seam allowance, directly across from where the thread came out of the first fabric.

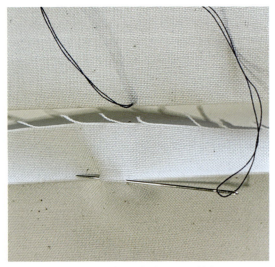

3. Bring the needle up through the second fabric approximately ¼" (6.4mm) away from the previous stitch.

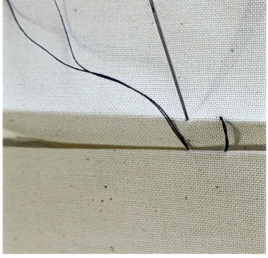

4. Take the needle down through the first piece of fabric directly across from where the thread came out of the second fabric.

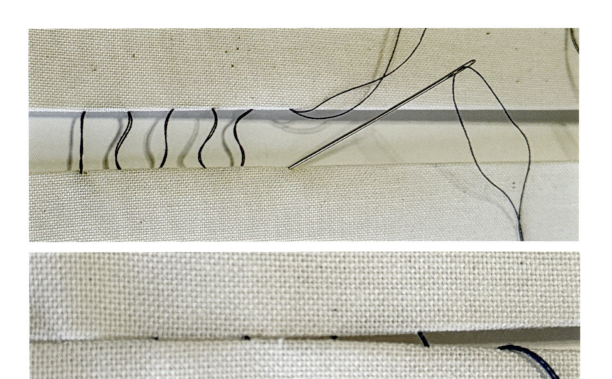

5. Continue repeating the steps above to create stitches directly across from one another in each fabric. When the stitches are pulled tight, the fabric will come together, and the thread will not be visible.

Tip!

Sewing buttons on a garment or project doesn't have to be boring! Use embroidery floss and decorative stitches to sew four-holed buttons in place.

Blanket Stitch

A blanket stitch is a stitch commonly used along the edge of a fabric. It can either be used as a decorative stitch or edging, or to hold layers of fabric together when doing a technique like appliqué.

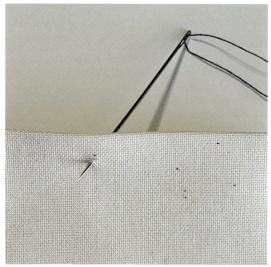

1. Bring the needle through the fabric from the wrong side approximately ¼" (6.4mm) down from the edge.

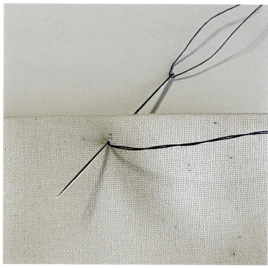

2. Make an anchor stitch by again bringing the needle through the fabric from the wrong side at the same point, wrapping the thread around the edge of the fabric.

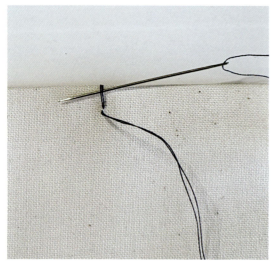

3. Along the edge of the fabric, insert the needle under the thread of the previous stitch, then pull the thread taut.

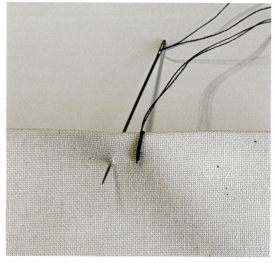

4. Take the needle through the fabric from back to front approximately ¼" (6.4mm) away from the previous stitch and ¼" (6.4mm) down from the edge.

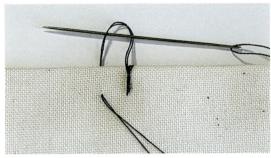

5. Pull the thread until there is a small loop, then insert the needle through the loop of thread.

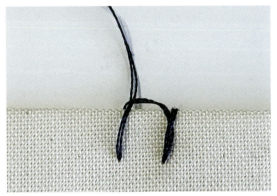

6. Pull the thread taut so that it lies flat along the fabric edge.

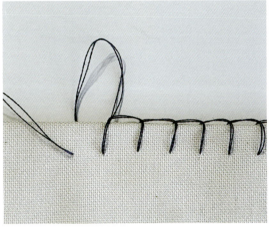

7. Continue repeating the steps above to take more stitches approximately ¼" (6.4mm) away from the previous stitch and ¼" (6.4mm) down from the edge, looping the thread through each stitch so that the thread lies flat along the fabric edge.

Trick!

A quick and easy way to keep hand blanket stitches evenly spaced along a fabric edge is to make marks on the finger you use to hold the fabric as you sew!

Hand Sewing / Hand-Sewing Stitches

Needle Knowledge

Choosing the right needle is key to successful sewing, whether by hand or machine. From delicate hand stitching to heavy-duty machine work, understanding your needle options will help you achieve cleaner stitches and better results in every project.

Machine-Sewing Needles 214

Hand-Sewing Needles............... 220

Machine-Sewing Needles

While all needles are made up of the same main parts, there are a variety of different types. Different needle types can be used depending on the application. There's pretty much a needle type for all fabrics and applications, which can make selecting one easy.

However, not everyone wants to own every type of needle out there, so know that there can be overlap and multiple uses within needle types. Understanding the different attributes of these many needle types will help you know what to look for when selecting a needle— meaning, it's less about what the needle is called and more about knowing when you need a rounded tip on a needle vs. a sharp point, or a large eye vs. a small eye.

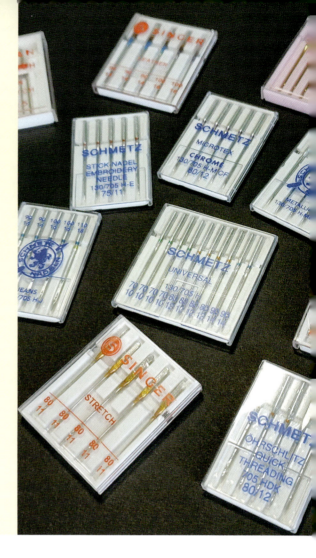

Tip!

A dull needle can lead to skipped stitches, thread nests, and other stitch quality issues. This is why it's important to change your needle regularly. If you are sewing a larger project, like a garment or quilt, it is a good idea to change your needle after every project. If you sew smaller projects, you can keep track of your sewing time and change your needle after roughly 8–10 hours of sewing. If you notice skipped stitches or other poor stitch quality, or you hear a "thumping" sound as your needle is trying to go through the fabric, it is definitely time to change the needle.

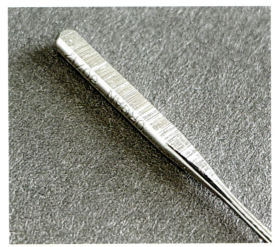

The beveled edge of a needle.

Anatomy of a Needle

Needles are made up of several main parts: butt, shank, shoulder, blade, groove, scarf, eye, point, and tip. Yes, that sounds like a lot of parts, but it's little changes to just one or two of these areas that set different needle types apart. And those changes are what help you get the best quality stitching on different types of fabric.

The butt is the very top of the needle. It generally has a beveled edge and is the part that gets inserted into the machine first. The shank of a needle is also inserted into the machine and can be where you see manufacturer information, whether that is a brand name or a color-coded reference to needle size. For home sewing machines, the shank will be flat on one side to indicate how the needle should be inserted into the machine—which is with the flat side toward the back of the machine. Commercial or industrial machines may have threaded or round shanks.

The shoulder is the sloped part of a needle between the shank and the blade. The blade is the body of the needle below the shank. The diameter of the needle

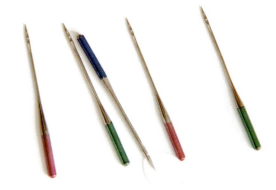

Some manufacturers will add a color-coded reference to needle size or type on the shoulder of the needle.

Needle Knowledge / Machine-Sewing Needles **215**

> **Tip!**
> Always thread your machine with the presser foot up, and only pull thread through your machine when the presser foot is up. When the presser foot is down, the tension disks are engaged, and pulling thread through the machine could harm those disks.

blade determines the needle size. The groove of a needle is what allows the thread to easily run along it and guides the thread to the eye of the needle. The scarf of a needle is the small indentation on the back of the needle that allows the bobbin hook to grab the thread and form a stitch. The eye of the needle is where the thread passes through. Finally, the point and tip of the needle are what penetrate the fabric and are different shapes and sharpness depending on the needle type.

Needle Sizes

Depending on the brand of needle you buy, you may see one or two different numbers, like 80/12. European sizes range from 60 to 110, while American sizes range from 8 to 18. The bigger the number, the heavier the needle.

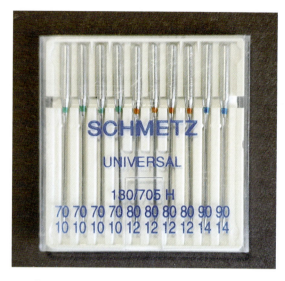

Universal Needle

Just as the name suggests, a universal needle can be used in all kinds of sewing applications and is one of the most widely used needles. Universal needles can be used with woven fabrics, synthetics, and even some knit fabrics. Universal needles come in a variety of sizes. The smaller/finer sizes are great to use on lightweight fabrics, while the larger/thicker sizes should be used on heavyweight fabrics.

> **Tip!**
> Not sure if your needle is the right size for the thread you want to use? Use this test. With the needle out of the machine, thread a length of thread approximately 15" (38.1cm) long through the eye of the needle. Hold one end of the thread in each hand with the needle at one end of the thread. Raise the hand closest to the needle up until the thread is at a steep diagonal. If the needle stays at that end of the thread, it is too small. If the needle immediately falls to the other end of the thread, it is too big. If the needle slowly slides or spirals its way to the other end of the thread, it is the right size.

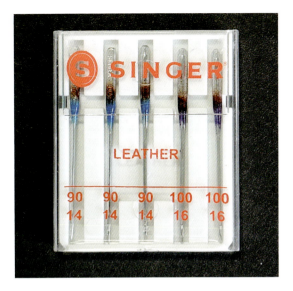

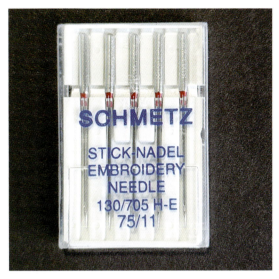

Leather Needle

Leather needles are specifically made to be used with leather or other very heavy or hard-to-sew materials. The point of a leather needle is triangular and looks like a small chisel. This enables it to pierce and pass through the leather without tearing or puckering the fabric as you sew.

Tip!

Let your sewing machine do the work! Never push or pull the fabric through the machine, rather allow the feed dogs to evenly move the fabric under the needle. This will help you maintain straight, even stitches.

Embroidery Needle

Embroidery needles have a larger eye and wider groove than other needles, which allows embroidery thread to easily pass through. This needle helps protect against thread breakage, especially given the speed and direction changes associated with embroidery.

Denim Needles

Denim or jean needles are specifically made to be used with denim and other heavy or densely woven fabrics. Denim needles have a very sharp point and a stronger shank to help protect against needle breakage.

Needle Knowledge / Machine-Sewing Needles

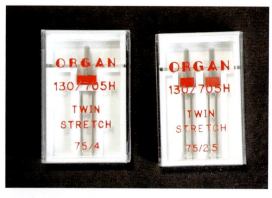

> **Tip!**
> A good rule of thumb when diagnosing poor stitch quality or other thread issues is, if the problem is happening on the underside of the work (for example, thread nests on the bobbin side), the cause is generally on the top. This could be either a dull needle, the wrong needle size or type, or an incorrectly threaded machine. Always make sure to check that your thread hasn't slipped out of the thread take-up lever when you start to stitch.

Twin Needles

Twin needles are essentially two needles on one shank. They can be used to stitch two parallel lines, for creating pintucks, or for other decorative stitches. Twin needles come in different sizes, indicated by the distance between the two needles. These needles are not always compatible with all machines, so consult your machine manual before using them.

Ballpoint Needles

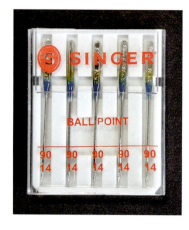

Ballpoint needles have a more rounded tip than other needles, which allow them to push the fabric fibers apart, rather than piercing through them. Ballpoint needles are great when sewing any kind of knit fabric as they help to avoid runs or snags happening along the stitching line.

Microtex or Sharps Needles

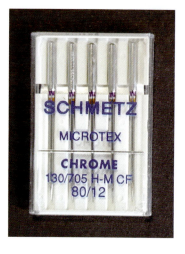

Microtex or sharps needles are designed to be used with densely woven fabrics or multiple layers of woven fabric. The slim point and sharp tip of the needle easily pierces through the fabric while the shorter eye and strong shank helps prevent bent or broken needles.

Quilting Needles

Quilting needles have a reinforced shank and are designed to stitch through multiple layers of fabric and batting. These needles are also shorter than other needles, allowing for quick and even stitches.

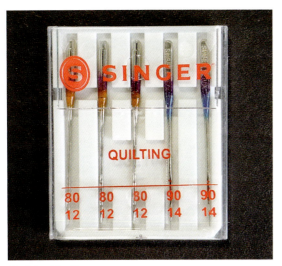

Quilting Needles

Metallic Needles

Metallic needles have an elongated eye to help accommodate metallic or other specialty threads, which help prevent shredding or thread breakage.

Hack!
Many quilters like using topstitching needles when quilting.

Stretch Needles

Stretch needles have a medium ball point and a deep scarf. The extra room on the scarf helps prevent skipped stitches on stretchy fabrics like stretch knits, jersey, and elastic.

Topstitch Needles

Topstitch needles have extra-sharp points and tips, which allow them to easily pierce through multiple layers of fabric while topstitching. They also have a large eye to accommodate thicker topstitching thread.

Quick-Threading Needles

Quick-threading needles are universal needles that have a slot in the eye allowing the thread to easily slide in. When using these needles, it is recommended that you reduce your sewing speed so that the thread doesn't pop out of the slot. Because there is an open slot on the back of the needle, avoid using delicate fabrics that could snag.

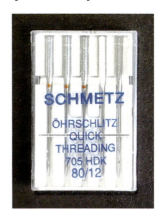

Hand-Sewing Needles

While hand-sewing needles might not be made up of as many different main parts as sewing-machine needles, there are still quite a few different types and sizes to choose from. As with sewing machine needles, there are hand sewing needles for almost every fabric type or application.

However, there is also overlap in uses, so again, you don't have to own every type of needle out there. If in doubt, choose a general-purpose or sharps needle, but know the different attributes of all these needle types so you can make your hand sewing easier and achieve the desired stitch quality by selecting the right needle.

Trick!

Any time you are hand sewing, whether it's embroidery or simply sewing on a button, use a thread conditioner or beeswax to keep the thread from knotting and tangling as you sew.

Needle Sizes

When it comes to hand-sewing needle sizes, the gauge or size of the needle is indicated by a number. The bigger the number, the finer and shorter the needle.

General Purpose: Sharps Needles

General purpose hand-sewing needles are the equivalent to a universal machine sewing needle. They can be used on a variety of different fabrics and come in a range of sizes for use on light to heavy fabrics. These are some of

Hack!

Putting together a travel mending kit and don't have a place to keep your needle? Store it inside a narrow spool of thread! Simply pull the bottom off the spool, place the needle inside, then slide it back in.

Tip!

If you need to change your needle because you are changing fabrics or the type of sewing you are doing—not because it is dull—rather than putting that needle back in the package, use a needle organizer pad. This will allow you to keep track of which needles are what size and type, while still ensuring that when you pull a needle from the package, it is always a new, sharp needle.

the most common needles used in dressmaking and tailoring. They have a sharp point and a short round eye.

Darner Needles

A darner is a sharp needle with an elongated eye. Darners are generally used for mending and come in a variety of sizes and thickness. There are both short and long darners, as well as yarn darners, which are used to sew wool or other thick fabric with yarn or other coarse thread.

Tapestry: Cross Stitch Needles

Tapestry needles have a large eye meant to accommodate tapestry thread or multiple strands of embroidery floss. These needles also have a blunt point,

Cross Stitch Needles

Chenille Needles

Quilting Needles

Milliners Needles

which allows the needle to push fabric fibers apart, rather than piercing through them. This prevents tearing or splitting of the fabric fibers.

Chenille Needles

Chenille needles are like tapestry needles in their overall length and diameter, as well as eye openings, but they have a very sharp point. This makes them a great needle for sewing or hand embroidery with thicker threads on linen or similar fabric.

Quilting Needles

Quilting needles are shorter needles that allow for faster stitching.

Hack!
Use masking tape or painter's tape to mark straight lines for quilting. Stitch along the edge of the tape and then easily remove it from the fabric.

Milliners Needles

Milliners needles are long, sharp needles generally used for pleating or other decorative stitching.

Leather Needles

Leather needles have a strong, sharp, triangular point that allows them to pierce through leather and other thick materials.

Embroidery: Crewel Needles

Embroidery needles have an elongated eye that allow them to accommodate thicker threads or multiple strands of embroidery floss.

Beading Needles

Beading needles are extremely fine needles with a small eye, allowing the

Crewel Needles *Beading Needles* *Collapsible-Eye Needles* *Easy Threading Needles*

needle to easily pass through beads, sequins, or other small embellishments.

Collapsible-Eye Needles

Collapsible-eye needles are fine needles commonly used in beading that have a large wire eye opening that expands for easy threading and collapses when pulled through beads or fabric.

Calyx Eye: Easy Threading Needles

A calyx-eye needle has a small slit in the top of the needle eye that allows the thread to slide through, making it easier to thread than traditional needles.

Curved Needles

A curved needle is a general-purpose needle that has a curve already bent into it. The curve makes it easier when doing repairs to upholstery or other projects where you may not be able to pull the needle all the way through to the other side.

Tip!

When sewing fabric that has sequins, beads, or other embellishments sewn onto the surface of the fabric, reinforce the embellishments by sewing them with a hand-sewing needle and thread along where you plan to cut the fabric before you cut it. This will eliminate embellishments falling off once the fabric and the thread holding them in place is cut. After a seam has been sewn, the embellishments can be removed from the seam allowance.

Thread Theory

Right up there in terms of importance with sewing needles is thread. Thread comes in all types of different fibers, weights, winds, and of course colors. Selecting the right thread for both the application as well as the needle and fabric combination can play a huge role in whether a project turns out well.

Thread Characteristics 226

Thread Types 230

Thread Processing 235

Thread Characteristics

Thread may seem simple, but its characteristics play a crucial role in the strength, appearance, and performance of your stitches. Understanding thread size, label numbers, and winding styles will help you choose the right thread for every fabric, technique, and project.

Thread Size and Label Numbers

Thread size is important to consider whether you are sewing, quilting, or embroidering. Similar to needles, thread size is noted by a number on the label. There can be a variety of different numbers on a label, depending on the thread type or manufacturer, and they note either the thread weight, tex, or denier.

While thread weight is technically how heavy a thread is, it is determined in part by a length measurement. Dividing a set weight of thread by the length it takes to reach that weight determines the overall thread weight. This means that a thread labeled as a 40 weight, abbreviated 40 wt., is because 40 kilometers of that

120D/2 means that this is made up of 2 plies of 120-denier thread.

12wt. means that 12km of this thread weighs 1kg.

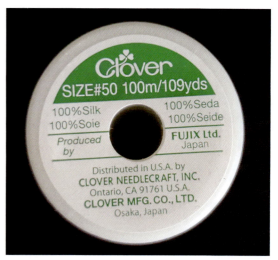

Size #50 is not the same as 50wt thread.

226   500 Sewing Tips, Tricks, Techniques, and Hacks

thread weighed 1 kilogram. This means that a thread that is a 50 wt. is lighter because it takes more of that thread to weigh one kilogram.

A tex number on a thread label is the weight of 1,000 meters of thread in grams. If 1,000 meters of thread weighs 30 grams, it is a tex 30. Heavier threads have larger tex numbers.

A denier number on a thread label is the weight of 9,000 meters of thread in grams. If 9,000 meters of thread weighs 100 grams, it is a 100-denier thread, often abbreviated 100D. Heavier threads are larger denier numbers. A denier number can also come with a second number associated with it, for example 100D/2. The second number indicates how many strands are in that thread.

It is important to know what type of number you are looking at when determining a thread size, because while larger tex and denier numbers mean that the thread is heavier, a larger number in thread weight means that the thread is finer. In general, thread weight is the most commonly used identifier of thread size, but it's always good to know what the other numbers mean if you see them on a label.

Wind

Thread can be wound onto spools in one of two ways, either cross wound or stacked. Cross-wound thread overlaps itself on the spool and creates small, elongated X shapes. Stacked thread is wound with all the threads parallel to one another. While both threads can

Cross wound (right) and stacked (left) threads.

Stacked threads work best from a vertical thread-spool pin.

Cross-wound threads work best from a horizontal thread-spool pin.

Thread Theory / Thread Characteristics   **227**

Tip!

If you want to use a cone of thread with a standard sewing machine, consider getting a stand-alone adjustable thread cone holder that can be placed next to your machine to hold the thread.

essentially be used the same, the main difference is their position on the sewing machine. Cross-wound threads work best when they are placed on a horizontal thread-spool pin, whereas stacked threads work best coming off a vertical thread-spool pin.

Spool Size

Thread can come on both cones and spools of various sizes. The amount of thread you need will ultimately decide the size of spool you choose to get. Both regular and slim spools can be used on standard sewing machines, while miniature spools should be saved for hand-sewing projects. Cones are more commonly used on industrial sewing machines, overlocker or sergers, or longarm quilting machines. These machines can accommodate these larger cones and have longer thread spool pins.

Tip!

If you have a thread that is too easily falling off the spool, or there is nowhere to secure the thread end when storing it, consider using a thread sock. Its adjustable net-like design will keep thread securely on the spool no matter the spool size!

Tip!

If you find that your spool of thread spins while you are sewing, which can cause the thread to get tangled below the spool of thread, use a felt or foam spacer under the spool. This will help hold the spool of thread in place.

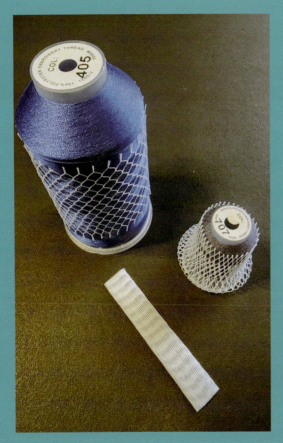

Tip!

Always use a thread-spool cap that is larger than the spool of thread. This will ensure that the thread does not get caught on the edge of spool as you sew.

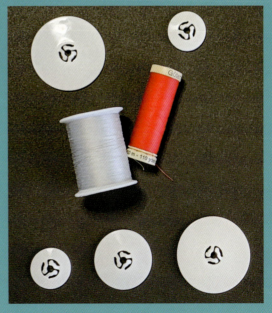

Thread Theory / Thread Characteristics

Thread Types

In addition to their weight and wind, threads come in a variety of types, which are generally associated with the natural or synthetic fibers that make up the thread.

Cotton Thread

Cotton is one of the most widely used thread types and is made from cotton fibers. Cotton thread is a strong thread that doesn't stretch, meaning it should be used on woven fabrics that also do not stretch. Like cotton fabric, cotton thread can fade and shrink when washed. This characteristic is one of the reasons why matching thread fiber content to fabric fiber content is a good idea, so that they react in the same manner.

Hack!

A silverware drawer tray can be used for storing spools of thread.

All-Purpose Thread

All-purpose thread is another widely used thread type because it can be used on a variety of different fabrics. All-purpose thread is generally either a polyester thread or a cotton-wrapped, polyester core thread. This allows the thread to be strong, while the addition of the polyester gives the thread some flexibility and protects against thread breakage.

Polyester Thread

Polyester is a very strong thread that has a small amount of flexibility. Unlike cotton thread, it will not shrink when washed, but it can only withstand moderate heat from an iron or dryer before its strength is diminished.

Metallic Thread

Metallic thread is a shiny thread commonly used in embroidery, topstitching, or any other application where the thread is readily visible. Metallic thread generally has a polyester core that is wrapped in metal foils. This thread is sometimes prone to breakage, so it is important to use a metallic or embroidery needle when sewing with this thread. You should also be careful not to use too high a heat on an iron around this thread as it could weaken it.

Rayon Thread

Rayon thread is a soft, shiny thread. It is not overly strong and is best used as an embroidery or other decorative stitch thread as opposed to construction. Rayon thread is best used with a fine sharps or Microtex needle.

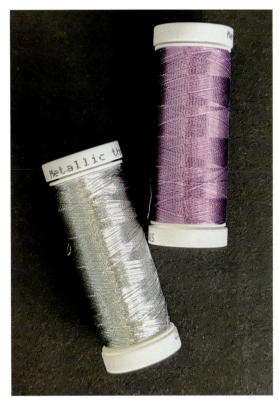

Mylar Thread

Mylar threads are made from thin layers of flat mylar material that are bonded together. It has a holographic or "glittery" look that can make for beautiful embroidery, topstitching, or other decorative stitches. Mylar thread is best used with either a metallic needle or a heavier topstitch needle, like a 90/14, that has a larger eye.

Monofilament Thread

Monofilament thread is also known as clear thread. This thread has a nylon base and resembles fine fishing line. It is a very strong thread that can be used when the stitches are intended to be invisible. Standard clear thread can be used on white and lighter fabrics, while the monofilament thread with a slight tint can be used on darker fabric. Monofilament threads work best with a sharps or Microtex needle.

Elastic Thread

Elastic thread is a thread type that should never actually be used in the needle of a sewing machine. Elastic thread can be hand wound onto a bobbin when gathering or shirring fabric.

Silk Thread

Silk thread is a very fine thread that is perfect to use when sewing with silk or other fine fabrics. It is strong, has some flexibility, and does not give off any lint when passing through the needle and fabric.

Embroidery Thread

Embroidery thread can be made from several different fiber types, from polyester to rayon to silk. Picking the right embroidery thread for a project can come down to what type of fabric is being embroidered. Lighter-weight fabrics work best with rayon and silk

thread, while heavier fabrics work best with polyester. Embroidery thread should be used with an embroidery needle.

Heavy Duty Thread

Heavy duty thread is exactly what it sounds like: a heavy thread that was designed to withstand stress and tension. This thread should be used on projects like luggage or sports gear where it could see lots of wear and tear. Heavy duty thread is best used with a heavier topstitch needle, like a $90/14$ or a $100/16$.

Denim Thread

Denim thread is another aptly named thread that is meant to be used when sewing jean or denim fabric. It is a heavyweight thread comprised of a polyester core wrapped in cotton, and like all-purpose thread, it is much heavier. Denim thread should be used with a denim needle.

Cotton Perle Thread

Cotton perle thread is a two-ply twisted thread commonly used with hand sewing and embroidery. However, unlike other

embroidery floss, the two-plies are not meant to be separated. It has a high sheen, which is why is it sometimes referred to as pearl cotton. This thread is very smooth and does not give off any lint when passing through the fabric.

Quilting Thread

Quilting thread is generally 100% cotton, though you can find some that are a cotton/polyester blend. Quilting thread has been mercerized, meaning that it was treated under tension to give it extra strength and shine. Quilting threads work best with quilting or medium-weight topstitching needles.

Serger Thread

Serger threads are generally finer than standard sewing threads. This is done to help reduce bulk on projects given that sergers use two or more spools of thread

when finishing a seam. This means that even with the finer thread, you will still have a strong seam because you have multiple threads.

Waxed Thread

Waxed thread is a thread that has been coated with wax to make it water repellent. While this makes it a great thread to use on outdoor projects, it is best used for hand sewing rather than with a sewing machine as the wax can build up in the machine. Waxed thread is also commonly used when hand sewing leather projects.

PTFE Thread

PTFE thread (polytetrafluoroethylene) or Teflon, is a thread that is both heavy duty and UV and water resistant, making it perfect for outdoor projects like camping gear or boating accessories. Because it is a very heavy-duty thread, it is best used with a heavy duty or industrial or commercial machine.

Thread Processing

In addition to the many different thread types, some of these threads can then be processed in ways that make them easier to sew with.

Mercerized Thread

Mercerization is a chemical treatment of a thread that increases its strength and shine. The cotton fibers are immersed in a caustic solution like sodium hydroxide. The solution causes the fibers to swell, allowing for better dye penetration and resulting in the increased shine or luster. Keeping the fibers under tension during this process also increases the thread strength and makes it less prone to shrinkage.

Glazed Thread

Glazed thread is a thread that has been heated and then coated with wax, resin, or other chemicals. This thread is very strong, but after being glazed it is much thicker and should be used with hand sewing as opposed to machine sewing. It is also not recommended to use glazed threads in a sewing machine as the wax or resin could rub off on the tension disks or other parts of the machine and cause buildup.

Gassed Thread

Gassed thread involves quickly passing cotton thread between two flames to burn off excess lint. This makes the thread smoother, which is also why this process can be referred to as silk finish or making a polished cotton.

Fabric Facts

Whether you are picking fabric because of a specific project you want to make, or you're trying to come up with a project for a specific fabric you found, fabric is still the foundation of every project. The easiest way to pick fabric for a project is to feel it. Is it heavy enough for a jacket, soft enough for a blanket, or does it drape well for a dress? While it's hard to get a real feel for fabric from a book, here are some fun fabric facts that might help you narrow things down the next time you are shopping for fabric. With a list long enough to include almost every letter of the alphabet, you might even learn about fabrics you never knew existed!

A

Acrylic Felt
Acrylic felt is a synthetic fabric commonly used in crafts. Acrylic felt is easy to sew by either hand or machine, and doesn't require any kind of seam finishing because it doesn't ravel. Because it is synthetic, it can melt if exposed to the heat of an iron, and ball or pill if exposed to the heat of a dryer.

B

Batik
Batik fabric is easily recognizable with its bright, vibrant colors and unique prints on both the right and wrong side of the fabric. Batik fabric is dyed using hot wax applied to the fabric as a resist. It is then dipped in the dye and the wax removed to reveal the pattern. The term *batik* technically refers to the dying process of the fabric, which is generally 100% cotton. Batik fabric is commonly used in everything from clothing to quilts to home décor.

Batiste
Batiste is a soft, lightweight woven fabric that is semi-transparent. Batiste is often mercerized, which gives it a sheen. It is commonly used for lightweight garments like blouses and lingerie.

Boiled Wool
Boiled wool is made by shrinking wool in hot water. It is a dense fabric with a felt-like texture. Because of how it is made, boiled wool is resistant to further shrinkage. The boiling process also makes it softer than other wool or felted fabrics and is more water resistant. Boiled wool is commonly used for outerwear like jackets, scarves, and hats.

Broadcloth
Broadcloth is a plain, tightly woven fabric. It is commonly made from cotton, rayon, or silk, and can be used for everything from clothing to home décor, and draperies to quilts.

Brocade
Brocade is a woven fabric with a raised design. It was originally made from silk, but today can be found made from linen, rayon, and other synthetic fibers. It has a very lustrous shine and is commonly used for fancier dresses and garments or draperies. Brocade tends to ravel easily, so keep that in mind when you are cutting pieces and be sure to finish all necessary seams.

> ### Trick!
> Working with a fabric that frays? Trim all edges with pinking shears to keep them from raveling while you work with them.

Burlap
Burlap is a heavy, coarse, woven fabric commonly made from fibers of the jute plant. It is a popular choice for bags, sacks, and other crafts or home décor. Because of its strength, burlap is also known to be used as packaging material, and in gardening and landscaping as a weed barrier.

C

Canvas
Canvas is a heavy-duty, tightly woven fabric generally made from cotton or linen. Because of its tightly woven nature, it is very strong and resistant to wear and tear. Canvas is commonly used for bags, backpacks, and sports and outdoor gear.

Cashmere
Cashmere is a type of wool made from Kashmir goats. It is finer than sheep's wool, making it much softer. Cashmere is commonly used in garments like sweaters, cardigans, and shawls. Because it is rarer than sheep's wool, cashmere is generally more expensive.

Chambray
Chambray is a lightweight, plain-weave fabric generally made from cotton or linen. Traditionally it was made predominantly in a light blue color, though nowadays it can be found in a variety of others. Chambray can have the look of denim fabric, though it is much lighter weight and breathable, making it a common choice for clothing like summer dresses, and men's or women's shirts.

Cheesecloth
Cheesecloth is a cotton gauze fabric with an open texture. Unlike most other fabrics, this one isn't often used for sewing or crafting. Cheesecloth is most often used in the kitchen for food preparation (and of course cheesemaking), as its open weave allows liquid to drain through while holding solid substances.

Chenille
Chenille is a soft fabric with a fuzzy texture that is typically made from a variety of fibers like cotton, polyester, rayon, and wool. It is commonly used for blankets, bedding, and upholstery, but can also be used for garments like sweaters or shawls.

Chiffon
Chiffon is a lightweight woven fabric made from a variety of fibers like cotton, polyester, nylon, and rayon. It is semi-transparent with a soft texture, making it a common choice for fancy garments or lingerie. Chiffon frays and ravels easily, so be sure to finish all necessary seams.

Tip!
If you plan to pre-wash a fabric that easily ravels or frays, zigzag or overcast stitch the raw edges first. This will prevent the fabric from raveling in the washer or dryer.

Corduroy
Corduroy fabric is easily recognizable with its distinctive raised ridges or "cords." It is a woven fabric, typically made from cotton fibers, that is thick, durable, and soft. Corduroy is commonly used for garments like shirts, pants, and jackets, and can also be used for upholstery.

Cotton
Cotton fabric is a natural cloth made from the fibers of the cotton plant. It is one of the most common and versatile fabrics and is used in several other textiles. Cotton is used for everything from garments to quilts, and bedding to home décor.

Crepe
Crepe is a woven fabric with a distinctive "wrinkled" look. It is made from a variety of fibers like cotton, silk, or synthetic blends. Crepe has a soft feel and is a breathable fabric, making it a common choice for dresses and blouses.

D

Damask
Damask is a woven fabric known for intricate designs and for being reversible. It is made from a variety of fibers like cotton, wool, or silk, and it is commonly either a tone-on-tone or two-tone coloration. Damask can be used for everything from clothing to upholstery, accessories to home décor, and even table settings and napkins.

Denim
Denim is a very sturdy, heavy-duty woven fabric typically made from cotton and dyed with indigo. It is a sturdy, durable fabric commonly used for jeans and jackets.

Dobby
Dobby is a woven fabric with distinctive geometric patterns. It is made on a dobby loom, which raises and lowers specific warp threads to create designs. It is made from a variety of fibers, like cotton, linen, silk, wool, and polyester. Dobby can be used for both clothing and home décor projects.

Duck Cloth
Duck cloth, also called duck canvas, is a heavy-duty woven fabric. It is more tightly woven than regular canvas, making it stronger and more durable. Duck cloth is commonly used for duffle bags, outdoor gear, or workwear garments.

Dupioni Silk
Dupioni silk is a tightly woven silk fabric with a lustrous sheen. Because of its tightly woven nature, it is heavier than other silk fabric and is a common choice for elegant dresses or similar garments.

E

Eyelet
Eyelet fabric is easily recognized with its small, patterned holes. These holes are reinforced with embroidery and will not ravel. Eyelet fabric is commonly made from cotton and is used for summer or other lightweight garments like dresses, skirts, and shirts.

Trick!
When hemming jeans or other garments made from bulky fabric, cut the seam allowance so that it can be pressed open. This will help even out the bulk.

Given the holes in the fabric design, it is also commonly used as an outer or decorative layer over another fabric.

F

Faux Fur
Faux fur is a synthetic fabric made to look like real fur. It is commonly made from acrylic or polyester, making it durable and easy to dye. Faux fur is used for everything from garments to home décor, and accessories.

Tip!
When sewing faux fur, shave away the fibers from the seam allowance using a razor. This will help reduce bulk from the seams and help them lay flatter.

Flannel
Flannel is a loosely woven fabric commonly known for its plaid pattern. It is mostly made from cotton, though it can also be made from other synthetic fibers. Flannel is a soft, warm, medium-weight fabric, making it a great choice for clothing and blankets.

Fleece
Fleece is a soft, synthetic fabric typically made from polyester. Fleece is warm, water resistant, and breathable, making it a great choice for outerwear.

Tip!
When making garments from a print fabric with any kind of horizontal line, be sure to line up the fabric print before cutting pieces two at a time, for example two shirt fronts, so that they are aligned when the garment is constructed.

You should also align the fabric pattern on pieces of the garment that come together, like the front pattern pieces of a shirt. To do this, with the fabric either right or wrong sides together, reposition the fabric along the folded edge so that the pattern on the top layer of fabric is perfectly aligned with the bottom layer and then pin in place. Place the shirt pattern piece on the fabric and cut out both layers at the same time.

Fabric Facts **241**

G

Gauze
Gauze is a loosely woven, lightweight fabric commonly made from cotton. Gauze is thin, soft, and breathable, and while commonly used for summer clothing it is also used for first-aid applications.

Georgette
Georgette is a lightweight, sheer fabric commonly made from silk. It has a dull or matte finish, or can even look like it has a "crinkled" surface. It is a common choice for garments like blouses or dresses.

Gingham
Gingham is a woven fabric known for its two-color checkered pattern. It is a medium-weight fabric usually made from cotton or a cotton blend, and it is a reversible pattern. Traditionally, the most common colors of gingham fabric were red and white or blue and white, though it can now be found in many different colors.

H

Haircloth
Haircloth is a stiff, woven cloth made using hair and fibers from animals like horses, goats, and rabbits. It is made using the coarser outer coats of these animals which makes the fabric stiff and rigid. Haircloth is used in upholsteries and carpets, and narrow strips of it can be used as stiffeners along garment edges like skirts where you want to maintain a certain shape.

J

Jersey
Jersey is a soft, stretchy knit fabric. It can be made from a variety of fibers like cotton, wool, or polyester. The fiber type, or combination of fibers, will determine the jersey's total amount of stretch and durability, but overall, jersey is a common fabric choice for t-shirts, sleepwear, and even bedding.

K

Knit
Knit fabric is made by interconnecting loops of thread or yarn. This manufacturing process results in a soft, stretchy fabric. Knit fabric can be made from cotton, wool, rayon, or linen. Some manufacturers will also add synthetic materials like spandex to increase the stretch of the fabric.

Tip!
Solid jersey knit fabrics tend to look the same on both the right and wrong side of the fabric. But, if you ever need to know which one is which, gently pull the fabric along the crosswise grain. The fabric will generally roll toward the right side.

Tip!

Know how much your knit fabric is going to stretch before you sew it! To determine the amount of stretch in a knit fabric, cut a 4" (10.2cm) length of the fabric. Stretch the fabric and remeasure. How much larger the fabric is equals the amount of stretch it has. For example, if the fabric now measures 5" (12.7cm), it has 25% stretch. If it now measures 6" (15.2cm), it has 50% stretch, and if it now measures 7" (17.8), it has 75% stretch.

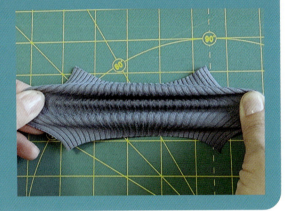

L

Lace
Lace is an openwork fabric with delicate patterns separated by spaces of open interlaced thread. Traditionally, lace was made from silk or linen, but can now be found in cotton or synthetic fibers. Because of the openwork design of lace, it is most used as an overlay on top of other fabrics, or used as an embellishment.

Laminated Cotton
Laminated cotton is a cotton fabric that has been coated with polyurethane laminate on the right side. The right side of the fabric becomes water resistant, while the wrong side of the fabric remains soft. Laminated cotton can be used for outer garments and is also a common choice when making a project like a makeup bag where you may want to easily wipe the fabric clean.

Lawn
Lawn is a lightweight, woven fabric made from cotton. It is thin, breathable, and fairly wrinkle resistant, making it a great choice for garments.

Leather
Leather is a fabric made from the hide of animals. It is heavy-duty, durable, and

flexible. Leather can be used in everything from garments to shoes, and upholstery to home décor.

Linen
Linen is a woven fabric made from the flax plant. It is lightweight, strong, and durable. Linen is a common choice for bedding, pillowcases, and towels, but can also be used for garments.

M

Mesh
Mesh is a fabric that can be either knit or woven and is easily recognized with its open, even, net-like spaces. It is commonly made from nylon or polyester and is a great choice for sports bags and outdoor bug netting.

Microfiber
Microfiber is created from ultra-fine synthetic fibers like polyester, acrylic, and viscose. It is

Fabric Facts

Trick!

One way to quickly and easily get a woven fabric edge on grain is to make a small clip along the selvage and then pull and tear the fabric. The fabric will naturally tear along the straight of grain.

Muslin
Muslin is a loosely woven cotton fabric. It is soft and breathable, and while commonly found in a beige or off-white color, it takes to dye well. Muslin is a common fabric choice for garment prototypes, which lead to those test garments being referred to as a "muslin."

Trick!

Another way to easily find the straight of grain in a woven fabric is to make a small clip along the selvage edge and then use a straight pin to help you separate one of the threads from the selvage edge. Pull on this thread until it breaks. This will create a visible line on the straight of grain that you can then cut along.

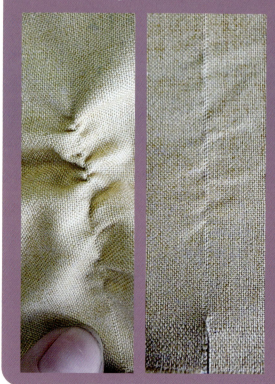

lightweight and has a very soft feel. It can be used in everything from garments to cleaning products.

Minky
Minky is a type of microfiber fabric typically made from 100% polyester. It is durable and has an ultra-soft feel. Minky can have a flat surface or be found with recognizable "dots" of raised texture.

Modal
Modal is a semi-synthetic fabric made from the pulp or cellulose of beech trees. It is soft, breathable, and absorbent, making it a great choice for undergarments, activewear, and even bedding.

N

Neoprene
Neoprene is a synthetic rubber fabric. It is made by layering either sheets of nylon, polyester, or acrylic on either side of a polychloroprene center. There are two versions of this center, one that is breathable, making fabric commonly used in outer garments or accessories, and one that is waterproof, making fabric commonly used in wetsuits.

Nylon
Nylon is a man-made synthetic fabric known for being durable and water-resistant. It is commonly used for raincoats, umbrellas, parachutes, camping equipment, and more.

O

Oilcloth
Oilcloth is a woven cotton or linen fabric coated with boiled linseed oil, which makes it waterproof. It is soft and flexible. Oilcloth is commonly used to make tablecloths, place mats, or reusable food bags.

Organza
Organza is a thin, woven, sheer fabric. Traditionally it was made from silk, but it is now made from synthetic fibers like polyester or nylon. Organza has a slippery surface, which can make it tricky to sew. It is commonly used to add structure to garments or fullness to skirts.

P

Polyester
Polyester is a synthetic fabric derived from petroleum-based chemicals. It is durable, wrinkle-resistant, and colorfast. Polyester is used in everything from clothing to accessories, home décor and carpets.

Poplin
Poplin is a woven fabric, typically made from cotton, wool, or silk, that features fine horizontal ribs of texture. It has a soft, luxurious feel and is a common choice for shirts, dresses, and sportswear.

Q

Quilted
Quilted fabric is two layers of fabric with a layer of batting or wool in the middle that is pre-quilted, generally in a square or diamond grid pattern. It is commonly used for jackets, tote bags, and upholstery.

Fabric Facts

R

Rayon
Rayon is a semi-synthetic fabric made from cellulose found in wood pulp. It is soft, smooth, and has a shiny appearance. Rayon is strong and breathable, making it a good choice for all kinds of garments.

S

Sateen
Sateen is a densely woven fabric made using a satin weave. It is commonly made from cotton, but can also be found made with wool or polyester. Sateen is soft and smooth. On one side sateen is matte and on the other it has a slight shine.

Satin
Satin is a fabric made from silk, polyester, or rayon using a satin weave. It is soft and smooth. Satin is matte on one side and shiny on the other. It is a common choice for evening gowns, ties, and linings.

Seersucker
Seersucker is a lightweight, woven fabric typically made from cotton, linen, silk, or a combination of the three. It features alternating smooth and puckered stripes and is a common choice for garments.

Silk
Silk is a woven fabric made from the natural protein fiber produced by silkworms. It is durable, smooth, and has a lustrous shine. Silk is also hypoallergenic and repels mold and bacteria. It is commonly used for dresses, ties, blouses, and other garments.

> ### Trick!
> If you're struggling to sew with slinky or slippery fabric, place a piece of tissue paper under the fabric layers before sewing. If needed, another layer of tissue paper can even be added to the top. The paper will help keep the fabric from moving as you sew and can easily be torn away after.

Spandex
Spandex is a synthetic fiber made primarily from polyurethane mixed with polyester or nylon. It is known for its high elasticity, making it a common choice for swimwear and other athletic apparel.

Suede
Suede is a type of leather fabric made from the underside of animal hides, typically lamb. It is thinner and softer than regular leather, but not as strong. Suede is breathable, making it a common choice for jackets and other garments. It is also water resistant, making it a common choice for upholstery.

T

Taffeta
Taffeta is a tightly woven fabric made from a variety of fibers, like silk, rayon, nylon, or polyester. It has a stiff, starched appearance, making it sturdy and able to hold its shape

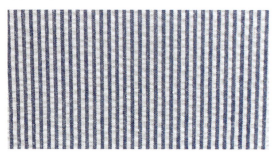

well. Taffeta is commonly used in garments like wedding dresses and corsets.

Terrycloth
Terrycloth is a knit fabric that has a smooth feel on the right side and soft fiber loops on the inside. It is commonly made from cotton, but can also be combined with polyester or rayon. Terrycloth is soft, breathable, and absorbent, making it a common choice for sweat shirts and pants.

Tulle
Tulle is a net-like, sheer fabric made from fibers like cotton, silk, nylon, or rayon. It is a lightweight fabric that is commonly stiffened to add fullness to wedding gowns or make things like veils or tutus.

Tweed
Tweed is a closely woven fabric made from wool. It is durable, warm, and water resistant, making it a common choice for jackets and other outerwear.

Twill
Twill is a woven fabric made from either cotton, wool, or silk. It is recognizable by its diagonal or ribbed pattern. Twill is a heavyweight, durable fabric commonly used in trousers, shirts, and jackets.

U

Ultrasuede
Ultrasuede is a synthetic microfiber fabric. It is made from fine polyester fibers and elastic polymers. Ultrasuede is durable, stain resistant, and easy to clean, making it a common choice for upholstery and automotive interiors.

V

Velour
Velour is a knit fabric made from polyester, cotton, spandex, or a blend of multiple fibers. It is a soft, moderately durable fabric with a sheen. Velour is commonly used for sportswear garments, drapes, upholstery, and blankets.

Velvet
Velvet is a densely woven fabric traditionally made from silk, but can now be found made from linen, cotton, wool, or synthetic fibers. It is soft, smooth, and has a shiny appearance. Velvet is commonly used for formal wear like

> ## *Tip!*
> When sewing a knit to a woven fabric, sew with the knit fabric on the bottom. This will help keep the knit fabric from being stretched by the pressure of the presser foot and will make for a much nicer seam.

Tip!

When sewing with vinyl, faux leather, or similar fabric, use binder clips rather than pins to secure the fabric. Pins can leave holes in the fabric that will not go away. However, if you must use pins on vinyl fabric because a binder clip or tape will not work in the given application or placement of a piece, pin directly in the seam line so that the hole left by the pins will be covered up with thread from sewing.

Tip!

On vinyl, faux leather, or similar fabric, use a permanent double-sided fabric tape and a seam roller to keep the outer edge of wider seam allowances flat.

1. Place the tape along the outer edge of the seam allowance.

2. Remove the paper backing and fold seam flat. Use the seam roller to ensure that the tape is securely adhered.

3. Topstitch the seam as desired. Placing the tape along the outer edge of the seam allowance leaves space for topstitching along the seam without stitching through the sticky tape.

evening dresses and gowns, but can also be used for curtains, upholstery, and pillows.

Vinyl
Vinyl is a synthetic fabric made from PVC, or polyvinyl chloride. It has a plastic-like feel and can be tricky to sew with, as it tends to "stick" to standard sewing machine presser feet. Vinyl is durable and easy to clean, making it a great choice for awnings or other protective coverings.

Voile
Voile is a lightweight fabric made from either 100% cotton, or cotton mixed with small amounts of linen, wool, or polyester. It is soft, sheer, and breathable, making it a good choice for summer or other lightweight clothing.

W

Wigan
Wigan is a cotton fabric commonly coated with a latex rubber or similar substance to give it stiffness. It is sold in strips and used to stabilize garment seams and hemlines.

Wool
Wool is a natural fabric made from the hair of animals like sheep, goats, or llamas. It is durable and warm, making it a great choice for clothing, specifically sweaters or other outerwear.

Wool Felt
Wool felt is a fabric made from matted and pressed wool fibers. It is warm, durable, and doesn't ravel. Wool felt is a common choice for accessories like mittens and hats, and is also commonly used in crafts or other home décor projects.

Woven
A woven fabric is made by interweaving two or more threads at right angles to one another. Woven fabrics can be made from either natural or synthetic fibers. They are generally durable with little-to-no stretch.

Z

Zephyr
Zephyr is a lightweight, woven fabric typically made from cotton. It is soft and breathable and is commonly used to make dresses and blouses.

Tip!
Looking for a solid fabric that will perfectly coordinate with your print? The selvage of the print fabric will have small circles with all the different colors that were used to make up the print.

Fabric Facts 249

Fabric Form & Function

While fabric types differ in what they are made from and how they are made, there are some general characteristics that apply to many fabrics, like pile, grain, and sizing. And while there are fabrics available that already have fun textures or embellishments, there are many ways to fold, gather, and create stunning patterns on the surface of a fabric.

Fabric Manipulation & Shaping Techniques 252

Smocking 264

Fabric Manipulation & Shaping Techniques

Fabric manipulation techniques allow you to shape, structure, and add dimension to your sewing projects. This chapter explores methods such as pleats, darts, gathers, and pintucks—each offering a unique way to control the fabric's form and flow.

Pile

Fabric pile, also called fabric nap, is the raised surface or texture of a fabric. It can be either strands of fibers or loops, and can be a variety of different lengths. Fabric nap is directional. To find the nap direction, simply run your hand along the fabric. The direction that feels the smoothest and has the fibers laying the flattest is the direction the nap goes. When making garments from fabric with nap, it is important to match the nap direction. This will ensure that the fabric across the entire garment feels and looks the same. Some fabrics, like velvet or velour, can look lighter or darker depending on which direction the nap is brushed.

Grain

Fabric grain is the direction of the fibers in a woven fabric. There are three types of grain: lengthwise, crosswise, and bias. Lengthwise grain, also known as the warp threads, runs parallel to the selvage edge of the fabric. These threads provide the most strength and stability in a fabric.

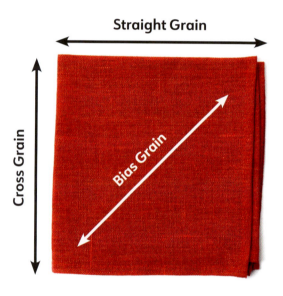

Crosswise grain, also known as the weft threads, runs perpendicular to the selvage edge. Bias grain runs at a 45° angle across the fabric. Bias grain is where a fabric has the most amount of stretch. When cutting garment pattern pieces from woven fabrics, it is important to align the grainline marking on the pattern with the lengthwise grain of the fabric. This will ensure that the garment fits and hangs correctly when worn, and has stretch in the correct areas.

Sizing

Sizing is a substance applied to fabric during the manufacturing process. It acts as a protective coating to help prevent breakage while a fabric is being made. Sizing can cause a fabric to feel stiff; however, it typically washes out once a fabric has been laundered.

Shirring

Shirring is a sewing technique that gathers fabric together, but still allows it to stay stretchy. It is used to add shaping and detail to garment areas like the bust or waist. To shirr fabric, parallel lines of stitching are made using cotton or all-purpose thread in the needle, and elastic thread in the bobbin.

Shirring is a technique that works best on light- to medium weight fabrics, as they gather easier and more evenly. Shirring will shrink the fabric where the lines of stitching are by approximately ¼, so keep that in mind when using this technique and start with larger pieces of fabric.

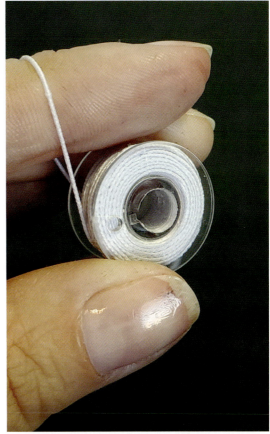

1. Wind elastic thread onto the bobbin by hand, never by machine. The machine, or even a stand-alone bobbin winder, adds too much tension to the elastic thread as it is wound. You want the thread to be slightly taut on the bobbin, but not pulled tight.

2. Tighten the needle tension. Most sewing machines have a tension knob or dial that can be set anywhere from 0 to 9. A general default position for the needle tension when sewing is in the middle, or around a 4. When shirring, you can adjust the needle tension to 7–9. You may need to run several lines of test stitches on a scrap piece of fabric first to determine the correct tension amount. The fabric should gather as you stitch. If it is not gathering, tighten the needle tension more. You will also need to lengthen the stitch length to 4mm.

3. Pull out and leave a long thread tail of both the needle and bobbin thread at the beginning of the fabric. Sew a couple stiches, then backstich one or two stiches. If your machine doesn't take well to backstitching with the elastic thread, you can use the long thread tails and tie them in a knot. Continue stitching a straight line across the fabric. The fabric will gather as you stitch. Backstitch or leave long thread tails at the end of the fabric and tie them in a knot.

4. Continue sewing evenly spaced parallel lines of stitching in the desired area of the fabric. As you sew, keep the fabric that is under the presser foot flat. The elastic thread will gather the fabric as it is stitched, but you don't want to purposefully stitch any folds or puckers into the fabric. You can pull slightly on the fabric to keep it flat as you sew. Note that you will see lines of the elastic thread on the wrong side of the fabric.

Knife Pleats

A knife pleat is considered a basic pleat and is essentially just a fold in the fabric. A knife pleat will take up three times its width in fabric, meaning it is three layers of fabric thick. So, for example, a 1" (2.5cm) knife pleat will take up 3" (7.6cm) of fabric.

1. Measure and mark the desired pleat width on the fabric. Start by marking the placement line where you want the pleat to end. Using the example measurement of a 1" (2.5cm) knife pleat, measure and mark 1" (2.5cm) to the left of the placement line. Repeat to measure and mark one more line 1" (2.5cm) to the left of the previous line. These two lines are fold lines. These marks can be made with a removable fabric marker or a hera marker as shown.

2. On the right side of the fabric, fold along the fold lines to form the pleat. The outer folded edge of the fabric should align with the placement line. Press in place and then pin or baste to secure.

3. Knife pleats can be folded in either direction. If you are following a commercial pattern, the direction that the pleats should be folded will be marked on the pattern with an arrow.

Box Pleats

Box pleats are made of two knife pleats folded away from one another on the wrong side of the fabric. They are used to add fullness to an area of a garment.

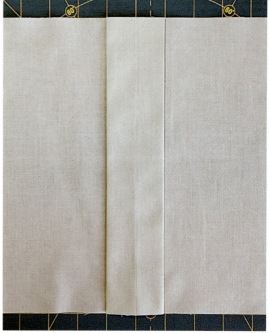

1. Mark where you want the center of the pleat to be. Using a 1" (2.5cm) pleat example, measure and mark 1" (2.5cm) to the right of the center line. Repeat to measure and mark one more line 1" (2.5cm) to the right of the previous line. Repeat again to mark two lines to the left of the center line 1" (2.5cm) apart. These lines are fold lines.

2. On the wrong side of the fabric, fold along the fold lines to form the pleat. The outer folded edges of the fabric should align at the center line. Press in place and then pin or baste to secure.

Accordion Pleat

Accordion pleats are simply rows of knife pleats all folded in the same direction. Because accordion pleats often go across an entire section of a garment, like around the waist area of a skirt, they are generally narrower. For example, rather than a 1" (2.5cm) pleat, they may be ½" (1.2cm) or less.

Twisted Pleat

A twisted pleat is a variation on a knife pleat. While a standard knife pleat is generally only secured at one end of the pleat, twisted pleats are secured at both ends and the ends are folded in opposite directions. These pleats can add a fun decorative element to garment areas like waistbands, or be used on other home décor or accessory projects.

To make a twisted pleat, measure and mark as if you were making a standard knife pleat. Ensure that you are making the marks on both the upper and lower edges of the fabric. Fold the upper edge of the pleat to either the right or left, then fold the lower edge of the pleat in the opposite direction. Press in place and then pin or baste to secure.

Dart

A dart is a triangular fold in fabric used to add shape to a garment. Darts are generally used in areas like the bust, waist, or hip of a garment.

1. Transfer the dart marking lines from the pattern piece to the wrong side of the fabric using a removable marker.

3. Starting at the wide end of the dart, sew along the drawn line, ending at the point. Backstitch to secure.

4. Press the dart to one side, or in the direction indicated on the pattern.

2. With right sides together, fold the dart in half so that the two lines of the dart are directly upon one another. Pin in place.

Tip!

When sewing darts on lightweight fabrics, do not backstitch. Rather, leave long thread tails at the beginning and end, and then hand tie knots in the thread. This gives a less bulky start and finish to the dart.

French Dart

A French dart combines a bust and waist dart into one longer, sometimes slightly curved dart.

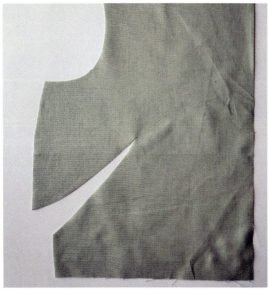

1. Transfer the dart marking lines from the pattern piece to the fabric, then cut along the dart lines.

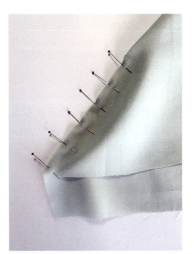

2. Align the raw edges of the dart and pin in place. Starting at the side seam, sew the dart together using a ¼" (6.4mm) seam allowance or the seam allowance noted in the pattern. Backstitch at the beginning and end, or, if using lightweight fabric, leave long thread tails and tie the thread ends into a knot.

3. Press the seam allowances to one side. Because of the slight curve of a French dart, it can be helpful to use a pressing ham (see page 19 for pressing ham).

Double-Pointed Dart

A double-pointed dart is a dart with two points. It is generally used to provide shaping to areas of a garment like a waistline.

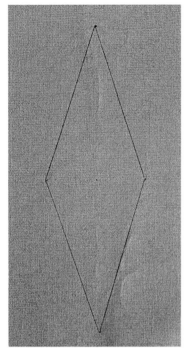

1. Transfer the dart marking lines from the pattern piece to the fabric using a removable marker.

2. With right sides together, fold the dart in half so that the lines of the dart are directly upon one another. Pin in place.

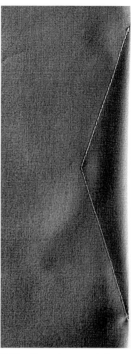

3. Starting at one point, sew along the drawn line, pivoting at the apex of the dart and ending at the other point. Backstitch at the beginning and end of the dart, or, if you are using lightweight fabric, leave long thread tails at the beginning and end and tie the ends into knots.

Trick!

When creating gathers on heavier fabric, where you are afraid the thread could break when being pulled, zigzag stitch over a length of floss, then pull on the floss to gather the fabric. Once the gather has been stitched into the garment or project, the floss can be removed.

Gather

A gather is simply bunching fabric together along a length of thread. This can be done with a gathering attachment on a machine, or by hand.

1. Lengthen the stitch length to 4mm. Leave long thread tails at the beginning of the fabric, then stitch a line of stitching within the seam allowance of the project you are making. For example, if you are sewing a garment with a ⅝" (1.6cm) seam allowance, run the line of gathering stitching ½" (1.2cm) from the fabric edge. Leave long thread tails at the end of the fabric as well.

2. Starting at one end, hold onto the bobbin thread and slowly pull the fabric toward the center to gather it. Work in small sections and don't pull too hard, as you don't want to break the thread. Tie the thread ends into a knot, then repeat the process from the other side to gather the remainder of the fabric. Gathering from both sides toward the center can help evenly distribute the fullness of the gather.

Tip!

If you need to pull the bobbin thread up through the throat plate to start a seam, like for a gather, pull out a length of needle thread and hold onto the end as you rotate the hand wheel of the machine toward yourself. The bobbin thread will catch on the needle thread. Gently pull on the needle thread to bring the bobbin thread up through the throat plate, then pull out the desired length.

A gather can be used on the waist area of a garment to create fullness.

Ruche

A ruche is essentially a gather in fabric. One of the main differences between gathering and ruching is where they are used on a garment. For example, a gather can be used on the waist area of a garment to create fullness. These gathers run parallel to the body.

Ruching can be found on sleeves, bodices, or skirts, and is a small gather mainly used as an embellishment. They can run either parallel or perpendicular to the body.

A ruched seam.

Ruching can be done by either sewing a straight line of stitching and pulling on one of the threads, like a gather, or by sewing a narrow strip of elastic to the wrong side of the fabric or seam.

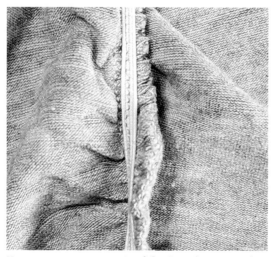

You can sew a narrow strip of elastic to the wrong side of the fabric or seam to create ruching.

Pintucks

Pintucks are very narrow tucks sewn into fabric and are generally used as decorative elements.

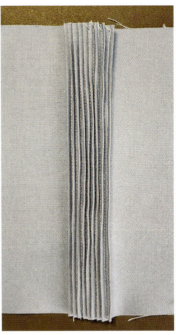

1. To create pintucks, draw spaced lines on the right side of your fabric using a removable fabric marker where you want the pintucks to be.

2. With wrong sides together, fold the fabric along one of the lines, then stitch approximately ⅛" (3.2mm) away from the edge.

3. Repeat to fold and stitch along all the marked lines.

Trick!

Pintucks can be easily sewn using a twin needle! To do this, start by inserting the twin needle into the machine and threading it according to your machine manual. Shorten the stitch length to 1.5mm, then simply sew a straight line. The fabric will "pucker" as you stitch.

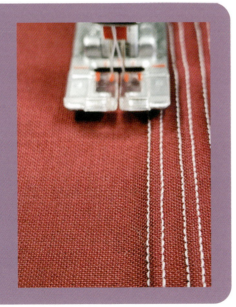

Fabric Form & Function / Fabric Manipulation & Shaping Techniques

Smocking

Smocking is a hand-sewing technique that involves pleating and sewing together small sections of fabric to create different patterns. Depending on the smocking technique you are using, the design can be purely decorative or can be used to add stretch to an area of a garment.

English Smocking

English smocking was traditionally used to add stretch or wearing ease to fabric. It is commonly recognized as rows of alternating grid-like hand stitching done on the right side of a fabric. There are several different stitches that can be used when smocking fabric, which will be shown below, but prior to stitching, the fabric needs to be pleated.

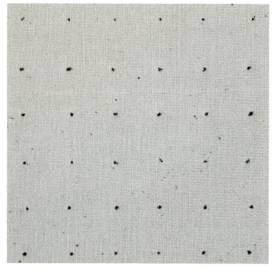

1. Mark a grid of dots using a removable fabric marker spaced ½" (1.2cm) apart across the area you wish to smock.

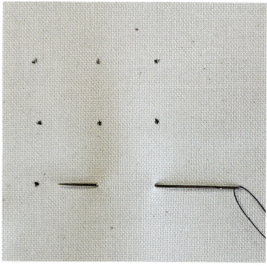

2. Thread a hand-sewing needle with a length of thread and knot the end. Place a running stitch along each line of dots, bringing your needle up through the fabric at one dot, then going back down through the fabric at the next dot.

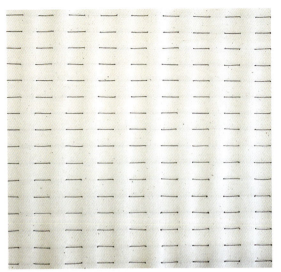

3. Repeat until there are lines of stitching across each row of dots.

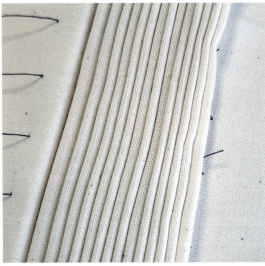

4. Gently pull on the end of the thread to gather up the fabric. The fabric will be evenly pleated. The upper folds of the fabric will be referred to as the peaks, while the lower folds of the fabric will be referred to as the valleys. The fabric is now ready to be stitched using your desired English smocking stitch.

English Smocking: Cable

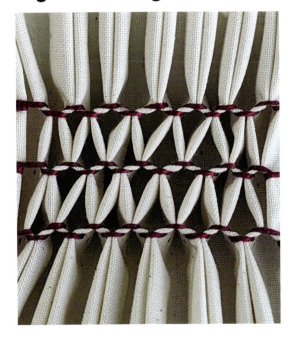

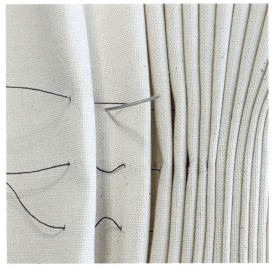

1. Thread a hand-sewing needle with a length of thread and knot the end. Starting at the left side of the fabric pleats, bring the needle through the fabric from the wrong side at the first valley. This will hide the knot on the wrong side of the fabric.

Fabric Form & Function / Smocking

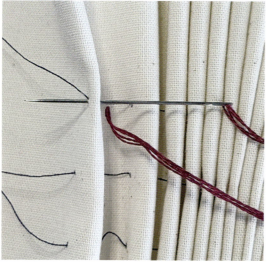 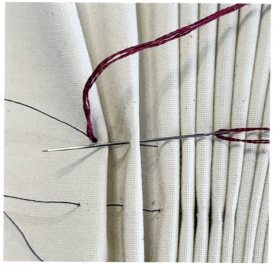

2. Stitching from right to left, insert the needle into the first peak of the pleated fabric, approximately ⅛" (3.2mm) from the upper edge and in line with one of the basting threads. Pull the thread taut.

3. Keeping the thread above the needle, stitch from right to left through the next peak in the pleated fabric, approximately ⅛" (3.2mm) away from the upper edge. Keep the smocking stitches in line with the basting stitches. This will help to keep the smocking stitches straight.

 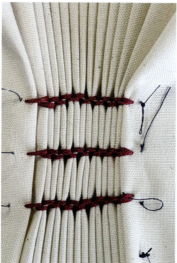

4. Next, keeping the thread below the needle, stitch from right to left through the next peak in the pleated fabric.

5. Repeat this process across each row of the entire pleated section, alternating between keeping the thread above and below the needle, and keeping the stitches approximately ⅛" (3.2mm) away from the upper edge. At the end of each row, bring the needle down through the last valley to pull the thread to the wrong side, and secure with a knot. Repeat for the desired rows of smocking. After all the smocking stitches are complete, the initial lines of thread used to gather the fabric can be removed.

English Smocking: Wave

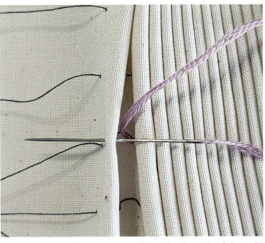

1. Thread a hand-sewing needle with a length of thread and knot the end. Starting at the left side of the fabric pleats, bring the needle through the fabric from the wrong side at the first valley. This will hide the knot on the wrong side of the fabric. Stitching from right to left, insert the needle into the first peak of the pleated fabric, approximately ⅛" (3.2mm) from the upper edge and in line with one of the basting threads. Pull the thread taut.

2. Keeping the thread above the needle, stitch from right to left through the next peak in the pleated fabric, ⅛" (3.2mm) below the previous stitch.

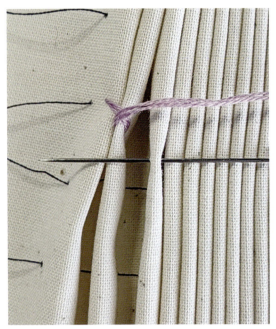

3. Again, keeping the thread above the needle, stitch from right to left through the next peak in the pleated fabric, ⅛" (3.2mm) below the previous stitch.

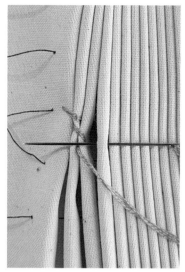 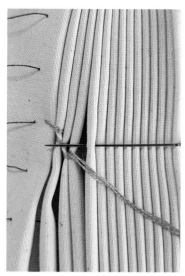 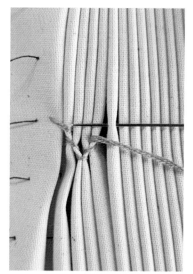

4. With the thread below the needle, stitch from right to left through the next peak in the pleated fabric, directly across from the previous stitch.

5. Keeping the thread below the needle, stitch from right to left through the next peak in the pleated fabric, ⅛" (3.2mm) above the previous stitch.

6. Again, keeping the thread below the needle, stitch from right to left through the next peak in the pleated fabric, ⅛" (3.2mm) above the previous stitch.

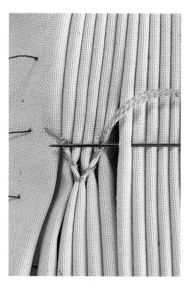 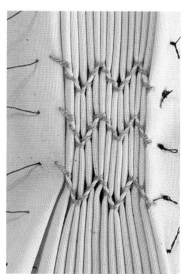 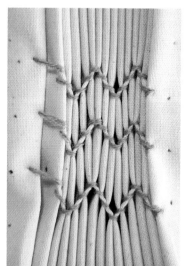

7. With the thread above the needle, stitch from right to left through the next peak in the pleated fabric, directly across from the previous stitch. This will complete the first wave.

8. Repeat this process across the pleated section, always keeping your thread above the needle as you work down the wave, and below the needle as you work up the wave. At the end of the row, bring the needle down through the last valley to pull the thread to the wrong side, and secure with a knot. Repeat for the desired rows of smocking. After all the smocking stitches are complete, the initial lines of thread used to gather the fabric can be removed.

English Smocking: Honeycomb

1. Thread a hand-sewing needle with a length of thread and knot the end. Starting at the left side of the fabric pleats, bring the needle through the fabric from the wrong side at the first valley. This will hide the knot on the wrong side of the fabric. Stitching from right to left, insert the needle into the first peak of the pleated fabric, approximately ⅛" (3.2mm) from the upper edge and in line with one of the basting threads. Pull the thread taut.

2. Stitching from right to left, insert the needle into the second peak of the pleated fabric, directly across from the previous stitch. Pull the thread tight to secure the first and second peaks, then repeat with a second stitch directly on top of the first.

Fabric Form & Function / Smocking

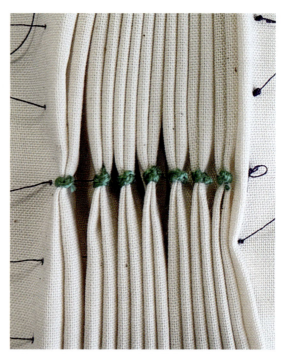

3. Insert the needle under the smocking stitches and pull until there is a small loop. Insert the needle into the thread loop and then pull tight to tie a knot. Repeat to make a second knot, then bring the thread through to the wrong side of the fabric and clip the thread.

4. Repeat the process to stitch all the peaks into pairs across the entire row of pleated fabric.

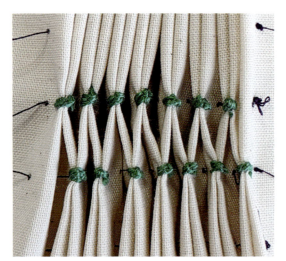

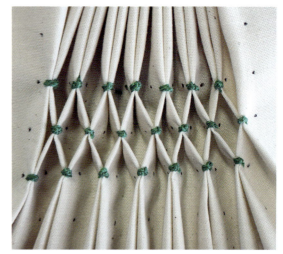

5. Repeat the process again on the next row down, but alternate the pleated pairs so that the stitching creates a V shape.

6. Repeat for the desired rows of smocking. After all the smocking stitches are complete, the initial lines of thread used to gather the fabric can be removed.

Canadian Smocking

Canadian smocking is a decorative hand-sewing technique that secures folds in fabric to create various patterns and designs. Unlike English smocking, where all stitching is visible, Canadian smocking is done entirely from the wrong side of the fabric. Also, Canadian smocking does not provide any stretch or give in the design area.

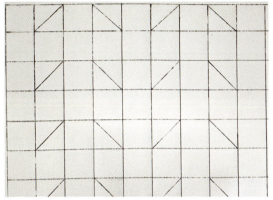

1. Draw a 1" (2.5cm) grid on the wrong side of the fabric in the area you want to add the smocking. For all Canadian smocking patterns, there are directional lines within some of the boxes of the grid. These are where the stitches take place. Transfer all directional lines from a Canadian smocking pattern to the grid on the wrong side of the fabric.

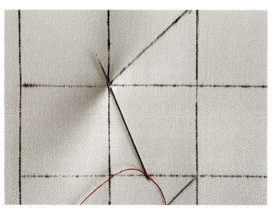

2. Starting at the upper left-hand side and working your way across each row to the right, find the first box with a directional line. With a knotted length of thread, take a small stitch at one end of the line in the corner of the square.

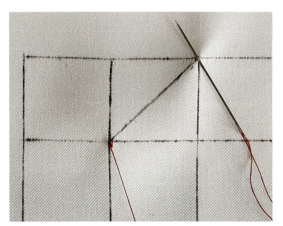

3. Take another small stitch at the opposite end of the line in the corner of the square and pull the thread tight to bring the two corners together.

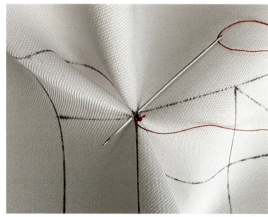

4. Take another small stitch over the previous stitch and tie a knot to secure.

5. Repeat the process to bring the corners of squares together anywhere there is a directional line in the grid. Lines can also extend across multiple squares, like in the bricks pattern below. You still bring the corners together at the ends of the line. Here are several patterns to try!

Canadian Smocking: Arrow

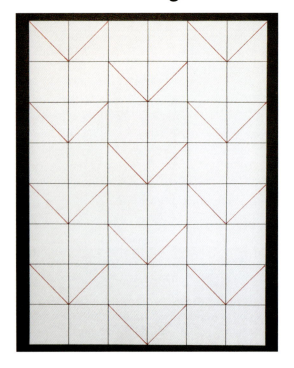

Canadian Smocking: Bones

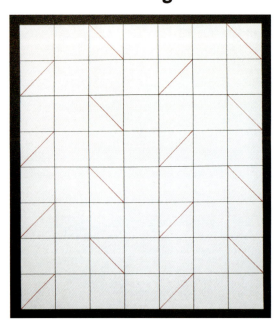

Canadian Smocking: Bricks

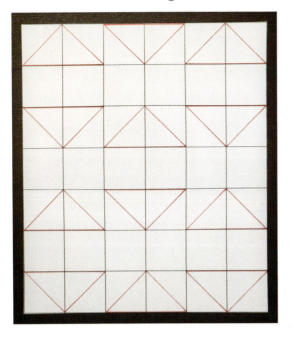

Tip! For a fun variation on this pattern, stitch the center of the brick together to turn it into a bow!

Canadian Smocking: Braid

Canadian Smocking: Heart

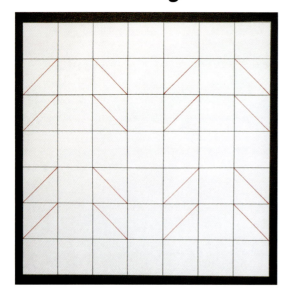

Canadian Smocking: Lattice

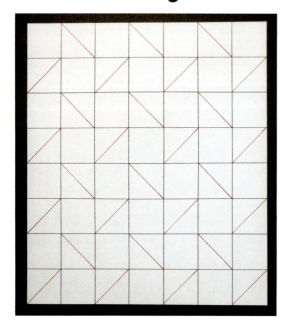

Canadian Smocking: Leaf

Canadian Smocking: Wave

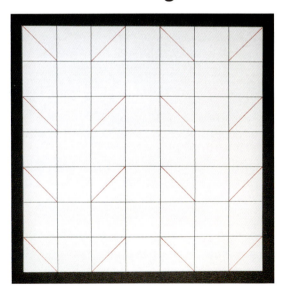

Index

accordion pleat, 257
acrylic felt, 238
air-soluble fabric marker, 13
all-purpose thread, 230
all-purpose zipper, 128
angled patch pocket, 50
angled pocket flap, 59
appliqué, 106; tip for, 107
appliqué pin, 8
appliqué scissors, 18
backing, binding from, 184
backstitch, 207
ballpoint needles (machine), 218
ballpoint pin, 8
bar tacks, tip for, 56
barrel cuff, 80
basting pin, 9
basting spray, 26
basting stitch, 207
batik, 238
batiste, 238
beading needles (hand sewing), 222, 223
bias grain, 252
bias tape maker, 25
binder clips (tip), 248
binding, 176–185; from backing, 184
blade (of machine needle), 215
blanket stitch, 210
blind hem, 159
blind-hem foot, 30
bobbin area: tip to avoid thread tangles, 23
bobbin buddies, 22
bobbin hacks, 112–113
bobbin winder, 22
bobbin winding (tip), 22
bobbin work, 110
bodkin, 24
boiled wool, 238
boning. See stiffened seam
bow, trick to tie a perfect, 108
box corners, 36, 38
box pleats, 256
braided elastic, 92
broadcloth, 238

brocade, 238
burlap, 238
butt (of machine needle), 215
button foot, 32
button, 144; on men's vs women's tops (tip), 153; sewing (trick), 60, 144; sewing with decorative stitches (tip), 209; storing (hack), 144; tip, 60; toothpick (tip), 60
buttonhole: invisible, 151; rectangular bound, 146; triangular bound, 149; trick for cutting open, 23; types of, 145; vertical vs. horizontal (tip), 145
buttonhole cutter, 26
buttonhole elastic, 93
buttonhole foot, 32
buttonhole spacer, 26
calyx-eye (hand sewing), 223
Canadian smocking, 271; arrow pattern, 272; bones pattern, 272; bow pattern (tip for bricks variation), 273; braid pattern, 273; bricks pattern, 273; heart pattern, 274; lattice pattern, 274; leaf pattern, 275; wave pattern, 275
canvas, 239; duck canvas, 240
cashmere, 239
chain piecing (tip), 51
chalk sharpener, 13
chambray, 239
cheesecloth, 239
chenille needles (hand sewing), 222
chenille, 239
chiffon, 239
circle cutter, 16
circles (on pattern), 120
clapper, 20
clipping corners, trick for, 173
clothespin hack, 106
collapsible-eye needles (hand sewing), 223
collar, basic, 86; cutting tip, 90; types of, 86–91

commercial pattern pieces: hack for, 122; tip to flatten, 123
construction techniques, 36–49
continuous bias binding, 176; calculating, 178
cording foot, 30
corduroy, 239
corners: clipping (trick), 173; mitered, 170–175; piping on, 199
cotton perle thread, 233
cotton thread, 230
cotton, 240
couching, 110
crepe, 240
crewel needles (hand sewing), 222, 223
cross grain, 252
cross stitch needles (hand sewing), 221, 222
cuff link, creating from shank buttons (tip), 84
cuffs, types of, 80–85
curved embroidery scissors, 18
curved needles (hand sewing), 223
curved rulers, 12
curved seam, 100; tip for sewing, 101
curves, piping on, 198
cut on fold line (pattern marking), 122
cut-away stabilizer, 96
cutting mat: rotating, 16; self-healing, 16
cutting tools, 15
damask, 240
darner needles (hand sewing), 221
dart, 258; double-pointed, 260; French, 259; sewing on lightweight fabric (tip), 258
decorative tape zipper, 129
decorative tooth zipper, 130
denim, 240
denim needles (machine), 217
denim thread, 233
dobby, 240

dog ears (on pocket), 53
double notch (on pattern), 118; tip for cutting, 101
double-fold hem, 156
double-fold tape, 164; sewing tip, 165
double-pointed dart, 260
duck cloth, 240
dupioni silk, 240
elastic thread, 232
elastic, types of, 92
elastic: inserting, 94; joining ends, 95
embellishments, 106, 192–201
embroidery needles: hand sewing, 222; machine, 217
embroidery scissors, curved, 18
embroidery thread, 232
English smocking, 264; cable pattern, 265; honeycomb pattern, 269; wave pattern, 267
eye tip (of machine needle), 215
eyelet, or grommet, 139
eyelet fabric, 240
fabric: coordinating fabrics (tip), 249; embellished, tip for cutting, 223; hemming bulky (trick), 240; matching pattern (tip), 241; marking or cutting (hack), 120; sewing slippery (tip), 246; stop fraying (tips), 238, 239
fabric glue, 26
fabric grain, 252; finding (tip), 244; cutting on (tip), 244
fabric manipulation and shaping techniques, 252–263
fabric marker: air-soluble, 13; heat-erasable, 13; water-soluble, 13
fabric pile, 252
fabric sizing, 253
fabric types, 238–249
faced hem, 158
fasteners, 139
faux fur, 241
faux leather, tip for sewing, 248
fiberglass measuring tape, 12
flange binding, 183
flannel, 241
flat sleeve insertion, 72

flat-felled seam, 186; tips for, 187
flat-head pin, 9
fleece, 241
flexible-head pin, 9
fold-over elastic, 93
fork pin, 9
Fray Check, 21
free-motion foot, 29
freezer paper, as template hack, 120
French cuff, 84
French dart, 259; sewing on lightweight fabric (tip), 258
French seam, 188
frog (fastener), 143
fusible bias tape maker, 25
fusible interfacing, 97
fusible web, 99
fusible-hem tape, 163
gassed thread, 235
gather, 261; tip for creating, 260
gauze, 242
general purpose (hand sewing), 220
georgette, 242
gingham, 242
glass-head pin, 9
glazed thread, 235
godet, 40
gore, 40
grain (fabric), 252
grainline (on pattern), 121
grommet or eyelet, 139
groove scarf (of machine needle), 215
guide bar, 29
guide foot, 28
gusset, 48
haircloth, 242
hand-sewing needles, 220–223; easy threading, 223; thread conditioner for (tip), 220; sizes, 220
hand-sewing stitches, 206–211
heat-erasable fabric marker, 13
heavy-duty thread, 233
hems, types of, 156
hera marker, 14
Hong Kong seam, 189
hook and eye, 142
hook-and-loop tape, 143

hump jumper, 24
inseam pocket, 66
interfacing, types of, 96
inverted box pleat pocket, 56
invisible buttonhole, 151
invisible hand stitch (ladder stitch), 208
invisible zipper, 129, 133
ironing board, 19
ironing, vs. pressing, 97
jersey, 242

joining binding ends: diagonal, 181; overlap, 180
knife pleats, 255
knit fabric, 242; right side (tip), 242; sewing to woven fabric (tip), 247; stretch (tip), 243
knit elastic, 93
knit interfacing, 97
knot, how to tie, 204; trick for tying, 205
lace, 243
lace-hem tape, 162
ladder stitch, 208
laminated cotton, 243
lapped seam, 191
lapped zipper, 134
lawn, 243
leather, 243
leather needles: hand sewing, 222; machine, 217
leather thimble, 10
lengthen and shorten lines (on pattern), 122
linen, 243
machine-sewing needles, 214–219; color-coded, 215; parts of, 215; sizes, 216; test for needle sizing, (tip), 216; tip for, 214

Index **277**

mandarin collar, 89
marking tools, 13
measurements, 124
measuring tape: fiberglass, 12; retractable, 12
measuring tools, 12
mercerized thread, 235
mesh, 243
metal thimble, 10
metal zipper, 128
metallic needles (machine), 219
metallic thread, 231
microfiber, 243
Microtex or sharps needles (machine), 218
milliners needles (hand sewing), 222
minky, 244
mitered corner: 90 degree, 170; borders, 174; double-fold hem, 171; easy, 168; tip for sewing, 171
mitered cuff, 83
modal, 244
molded plastic zipper, 128
monofilament thread, 232
muslin, 244
mylar thread, 231–232
needle organizer pad (tip), 221
needle sizing: hand sewing, 220; machine sewing, 216
needle storage (inside narrow spool tip), 221
needle threaders, 21
needle, anatomy of a, 215
neoprene, 245
nesting seams, 103; tip for, 103
netting, tip for cutting embellishments, 107
no-bulk stitch: join elastic ends with, 95
non-woven interfacing, 97
notches (on pattern), 118; tip for cutting, 101
nylon, 245
oilcloth, 245
open thimble, 11
open-toe foot, 28
openwork seam, 104
organza, 245
overcast foot, 30
pant slit, easy, 46

pants, tip for hemming, 125
partial seam technique, 101
patch pocket with piping border, 54
pattern drafting paper, 25
pattern, lengthening and shortening, 125
pattern markings, 118
pattern pieces (commercial): hack for, 122; tip for cutting, 61, 122; tip to flatten, 123
pattern sizes, grading between, 125
pattern weights, hack, 123
Peter Pan collar, 90
pincushion, strawberry on, 21
pinking shears, 18
pins, types of, 8
pintuck foot, 30
pintucks, 262; using twin needle (tip), 263
piping, 197; border for patch pocket, 54; joining ends, 200; on corners, 199; on curves, 198
piping foot, 30
pleats, 255–257
pockets: dog ears, 53; types of, 50
point-turning tool, 24
polyester thread, 231
polyester, 245
poplin, 245
prairie points, 193
press cloth, 20
pressing bar, 20
pressing ham, 19
pressing mat, 19
pressing tools, 19
pressing vs. ironing, 97
PTFE thread, 234

quarter marking, 94
quarter-inch foot, 28
quick-threading needles (machine), 219
quilted (fabric), 245
quilting needles: hand sewing, 222; machine, 218
quilting rulers, 12
quilting thread, 234
rayon (fabric), 246
rayon thread, 231
rectangular bound buttonhole, 146
retractable measuring tape, 12
reverse appliqué, 107
ribbon storage hack, 115
rickrack, 201; twisted, 201
ring thimble, 11
rolled hem, 157; hack for, 157
rolled-hem foot, 31
roller foot, 32
rotary blades: sizes, 16; specialty, 16; tips for, 16
rotary cutters, 15; tips for, 15
rotating cutting mat, 16
rounded cuff, 82
rounded patch pocket, 52
rounded pocket flaps, 57
ruche, 261
ruler, curved, 12; quilting, 12
ruler grip tape, 12
running stitch, 206; tip for, 206
safari pocket, 55
sateen, 246
satin, 246
scallops, 196
scissors, 17
seam allowance magnet, hack for, 39
seam finishes, 186–191
seam gauge, 23
seam measurement guide, 24
seam ripper, 23; cutting open buttonholes (trick), 23; tip for, 23
seam roller, 20, 248
seams, types of 100–105
seersucker, 246
self-healing cutting mat, 16
separating zipper, 129
serger thread, 234
set-in sleeve, 70

setting a seam, tip for, 102
sew-in interfacing, 97
sewing machine, cleaning: hack, 27; tip, 28
sewing machine feet: markings on, 33; types of, 27–33
sewing practice, tip for, 41
shadow appliqué, 108
shank (of machine needle), 215
shank buttons, creating cuff link from (tip), 84
sharps needles (hand sewing), 220
shirring, 253
shorten lines, lengthen and (pattern marking), 122
shoulder (of machine needle), 215
side-split hem, 160. See also pant slit, 46; skirt slit, 42
silicone thimble, 10
silk, 246
silk pin, 8
silk thread, 232
single notch (on pattern), 118; tip for cutting, 101
single-fold hem, 156
single-fold tape, trick for making, 9
size lines (on pattern), 121
skirt slit, easy, 42
sleeve placket, 74; with fabric strip, 77
sleeve pressing board, 19
sleeves, types of, 70–79

slit: pant, 46; skirt, 42. See also side-split hem
smocking, 264–275
snaps, 140; tips for, 141
snips, 18; hack for, 17
spandex, 246
specialty rotary blades, 16
square stitch: join elastic ends with, 95
stabilizer, types of, 96
stay stitching, 192
stay tape, 99
sticky thimble, 10
stiffened seam, 104
stiletto, 23
stitch-in-the-ditch foot, 29
straight grain, 252
straight pin, 8
straight-stitch foot, 27
strawberry on a pincushion, 21
stretch needles (machine), 219
suede, 246
swim elastic, 93
taffeta, 246
tailor's chalk, 13
tapestry needles (hand sewing), 221
tear-away stabilizer, 96
Teflon foot, 31
Teflon pressing sheet, 20
terrycloth, 247
thimbles, types of, 10
thread: characteristics, 226; dernier, 227; label numbers, 226; size, 226; spool size, 228; storage hack, 230; tex, 226; types, 230–234; weight, 226; wind, 227
thread conditioner, 22; hack for, 22
thread cone, tip for using, 228
thread processing, 235
thread sock (tip), 229
thread spool tips (machine sewing), 229
topstitch needles (machine), 219
topstitching, 192; tip for, 81
T-pin, 9
tracing wheel and tracing paper, 13
trapunto, 114

triangular bound buttonhole, 149
tulle, 247
turn a perfect point (trick), 98
turnback cuff, 85
turning a narrow tube (tips for), 178, 179
tweed, 247
twill, 247
twin needles (machine), 218; creating pintucks with (tip), 263
twisted pleat, 257
twisted rickrack, 201
two-way zipper, 129
ultrasuede, 247
understitching, 193
universal foot, 27
universal needle (machine), 216
utility pocket, 53
velour, 247
velvet, 247
vinyl, 248; tip, 248
voile, 248
walking foot, 28
wash-away stabilizer, 96
water-soluble fabric marker, 13
waxed thread, 234
welt pocket, 62
welt seam, 190
Western pocket flap, 61
wigan, 249
window zipper opening, 137
wool fabric, 249
wool felt fabric, 249
woven elastic, 92
woven fabric, 249
woven interfacing, 96
zephyr, 249
zigzag foot, 27
zigzag seam, 190
zigzag stitch: join elastic ends with, 95
zipper foot, 31
zipper opening, window, 137
zippers: sewing techniques, 130, 132–138; types of, 128–131; with basted fabric, standard, 132
zipper tab, 136

Index 279

About the Author

Ashley started sewing when she was a young girl, sitting on her mom's lap and learning from her as she made clothes and other projects for around the house. Over the years she has learned many different techniques and tricks, and made everything from bags to quilts, clothes to stuffed animals, and baby blankets to her own wedding dress.

Ashley enjoys teaching both sewing and quilting and has many video tutorials on National Sewing Circle, National Quilters Circle, and Craftsy. She has had several patterns published in magazines like Sew News, Sew It All, and Quilty, has done educational videos for companies like Olfa, appeared on Sew It All TV, and co-hosted a short series all about quilting.

When she isn't sewing or quilting, she's still crafting and enjoys crocheting, knitting, woodworking, or any kind of DIY craft.